PRAISE FOR *PAYING FOR LONG-TERM CARE*

"While most of us plan well for every other transition in life, preparation for our final phase is often neglected. This often results in hurriedly pieced together arrangements after a crisis arises. Ben offers an excellent guide and walks through almost every consideration for seniors as they age. An investment of time now will enhance life later for you or a loved one."

— Daniel Rexroth, President and CEO at John Knox Village

"Any family faced with the difficulty of making decisions about an elderly loved one's care should read this book. *Paying For Long-Term Care* offers a comprehensive step-by-step process to help families understand their options about choosing and paying for long-term care. I highly recommend it to anyone who is navigating the senior care journey and needs to make informed decisions about their loved one's care."

—Jeff Balleau, Founder of Transitions for Senior Living

"I have 25 years of experience in the senior care industry, and Ben does an excellent job clarifying the hard truths that families will encounter. This book is a very helpful resource for any family, and I look forward to sharing it with the families I work with."

—Roberta McArthur, Executive Director, One Good Meal

"This is a much-needed resource. Even though I have been practicing elder law for over 15 years, I have few real answers for clients in need of guidance with long-term care arrangements. This area is complicated and hard to navigate, especially in a crisis. After hours of research and endless conversations, families still feel like they don't have options. This book will help so many people and save them thousands of dollars. I am excited to be able to share this resource with my own clients."

—Jennifer McKenna, Owner and Attorney at the The Law Office of Jennifer Ward McKenna

"Ben has made a very difficult process much easier to understand and shares his personal experience of the challenges of this transition. We all need to be better prepared to help accommodate our families when the time comes. Ben has empowered families with the knowledge they need, which will lessen the burden and allow them to focus on what's important. Thank you, Ben."

—Matt Sanning, Director, Lee's Summit Social Services

Paying For Long-Term Care

Paying For Long-Term Care

THE ESSENTIAL GUIDE TO UNDERSTANDING AND FUNDING SENIOR CARE

BEN RAO

Copyright © 2021 by Ben Rao

All rights reserved. No part of this publication may be reproduced in any form or by any means without written permission of the publisher or author, except in the case of brief quotations in critical articles and reviews.

Disclaimer: *Paying For Long-Term Care* is for informational purposes only.

This book is not a substitute for professional medical advice, examination, diagnosis or medical treatment. This book should not be used for diagnosing or treating a health problem or disease and is not a substitute for professional medical care. You should always seek medical advice from your doctor or other qualified health professionals before starting any new treatment or making any changes to an existing treatment. You should not delay in seeking or disregard medical advice based on information on this book.

This book is not a substitute for professional legal advice, and reading this book, or corresponding with the author does not constitute the formation of an attorney-client relationship. The choice of a lawyer is an important decision and should not be based solely upon advertisements. Past results are no guarantee of future results. Every case is different and must be judged on its own merits. This book may be considered attorney advertising under the rules of some states.

This book is not a substitute for professional financial advice regarding investments, annuities, real estate transactions, purchasing health insurance, or long-term care insurance. Reading this book or corresponding with its author does not create a fiduciary relationship or duty. All financial decisions, even supposedly conservative ones, involve some element of risk and should be considered carefully.

Published by Senior Care Advocate Books
www.payingforlongtermcare.com

ISBN (paperback): 978-1-954363-00-7
ISBN (e-book): 978-1-954363-01-4

Edited by David Aretha
Book Design by Christy Collins, Constellation Book Services

Printed in the United States of America

DEDICATION

To Grandma Birdie
Thanks for all the PB&Js.
Your homemade blackberry jam was the best.

Author's Note on the Front Cover Photo

Marie Rodgers, also known as Grandma Ree-Ree, passed on November 13, 2017 at the age of 91. Ree-Ree was my wife Rhonda's grandmother. She was caring and gentle and loved everyone. We all used to laugh that you could count on hearing a busy signal whenever we tried to call her. She would spend hours chatting on the phone with her two sisters and her many friends.

Ree-Ree loved flowers, gardening, and working side by side with her husband Roscoe on the farm. She was famous for her homemade bread, pancakes and cinnamon rolls (and all other carbs, now that I think about it). Simply put, everyone who knew Marie loved and admired her, especially her grandchildren and great-grandchildren. I couldn't think of a more fitting person to represent "family" in this guide to caring for our aging population.

It was a joy to know you, Ree-Ree. We all love and miss you.

CONTENTS

Making Decisions on Your Own Terms ... 1
Purpose: Here to Help You and Your Family ... 3
A Common Scenario: Meet Tom—My Stepfather ... 7

PART I

Chapter 1: The Facts—70% Will Need Care ... 17
Chapter 2: It's OK to Be Stressed ... 21
Chapter 3: Understanding Senior Service Providers and Resources ... 27
Chapter 4: Elder Law Attorneys ... 31
Chapter 5: Overview of Senior Living Options ... 33
Chapter 6: Staying at Home vs. Moving into a Senior Community ... 43
Chapter 7: The Cost of Long-Term Care ... 51
Chapter 8: Understanding Medicare and Medicaid ... 55
Chapter 9: Identifying Family Assets and Financial Resources ... 63

PART II

Chapter 10: How to Pay for Care ... 67
    SELLING THE FAMILY HOME ... 68
    VETERANS BENEFITS ... 76
    LONG-TERM CARE INSURANCE CLAIMS ... 81
    LIFE INSURANCE CONVERSIONS ... 87
    FINANCIAL RESOURCES FOR PEOPLE WITH CANCER ... 89
    REVERSE MORTGAGES ... 96
    HSA—HEALTH SAVINGS ACCOUNTS ... 99
    FUNDING STRATEGIES TO PAY FOR IMMEDIATE NEEDS ... 102

PART III

Chapter 11: Researching Senior Living Options — 111

Chapter 12: Making the Best Decision — 121

Chapter 13: Strategies for Successful Transitions: In-Home Care and Senior Living — 129

Chapter 14: How Technology Can Help with Companionship and Safety — 135

Chapter 15: Mental Health Resources for the Family and the Senior — 143

Chapter 16: Healthy Aging Through Nutrition and Exercise for Seniors — 147

Chapter 17: Planning for Your Future — 155

Chapter 18: Lessons Learned — 161

Additional Resources — 165

Making Decisions on Your Own Terms

When it comes to making some of life's biggest decisions about senior care, you may be thinking that you can delay and hold out longer. While this may be true, there will come a time when that's no longer the case. Like most things in life, it's easier to make decisions while the circumstances around you are still within your control. This is perhaps the most critical difference between a seamless process and one that spirals quickly out of control. By anticipating change and planning ahead, you can maintain control of situations even when confronted with life's often unpredictable changes.

Senior care services are designed with two key elements in mind:

- As a lifestyle enhancement to help seniors live as independently and safely for as long as possible
- Out of necessity due to a life-altering event requiring immediate intervention

Oftentimes, the latter dictates our plans for us. Regardless, the reality is that over 70% of all seniors will require care during their lifetime. Take a good look at the autonomy you have today and your hopes for the future. Use these goals to help you manage inevitable changes on your own terms and by your own design.

Purpose: Here to Help You and Your Family

Although this book is largely written for the adult family, I am strongly supportive of seniors who wish to maintain their own autonomy. Seniors should always be included in decisions about next steps in their life whenever possible.

This book offers you planning, ideas, and a roadmap that provides support and reduces time and stress when a parent or loved one needs senior care. Families and seniors are often ill-prepared for the transition not only emotionally but also financially, as many are unaware of how much care costs. Then there are the logistics: What do you do first? What are the options? Who can help? With this book's guidance, you can have confidence and peace of mind in the decisions ahead.

I just wasn't ready for my stepfather Tom's transition into long-term care, emotionally or logistically. I was even less prepared for the financial aspect of the journey.

I didn't know what assets my family had to pay for Tom's care.

I didn't know how to evaluate in-home care vs. long-term care.

I didn't know that Medicare would only cover a fraction of our expenses.

I didn't know how to apply for veterans benefits or if Tom even qualified.

I didn't know how to handle the house.

I didn't know how to research senior care options or where to start.

I didn't know what type of care would be ideal for Tom.

I didn't know how to determine which care community was right.

Simply put, I didn't know enough to know what to ask. My experience is not unique: It echoes that of millions of families across the country.

The Paying For Long-Term Care Process

Transitioning a loved one into senior care is often emotionally exhausting for families who may not be sure where to start, especially when a loved one needs care immediately.

Following the Paying For Long-Term Care Process will provide clarity and direction for families navigating the transition to senior care. Use this process to **assess** your loved one's care needs, **define** your financial baseline, **learn** the financial options available to you, **select** the best care option, and **transition** your loved one to care.

The Paying For Long-Term Care Process

1 ASSESS	2 DEFINE	3 LEARN	4 SELECT	5 TRANSITION
Evaluate your loved one's care needs	Identify assets and financial baseline	Discover financial resources available	Determine the best option for care	Move your loved one towards the best care

- Find an overview of care costs and options and learn how to compare them, as well as industry resources
- Learn the best way to search for care to save time and prevent unnecessary stress
- Understand your funding options and discover resources you may not have realized were available
- Utilize tips on coping with the emotional aspect of the journey, having important conversations with your loved one or parent, and on how to get the entire family onboard.

Once the decision is made and the finances are settled, a new journey begins: the transition. You'll learn how to make the transition go smoothly for your loved one or parent, and the entire family.

Lastly, we'll discuss healthy aging and the value in planning ahead. Most of us are guilty of taking our own health for granted. There are tips on preventative measures you can take to extend your independence while also making sure you're prepared for the future.

This book is committed to empowering families with information and resources to help you make informed decisions and get your loved one the care they need as quickly as possible. After you go through this experience with your parent or loved one, you'll have an entirely different outlook on aging and future care. And so will your aging loved one: Remember to include them in the planning process as much as possible. The ultimate goal is to remove some of the mystery and confusion involved with navigating senior care so that you can focus on being the loved one, not the caretaker.

There is only so much that can fit in a book, and it's impossible to cover every available option for your loved one's care. Throughout the book, I'll reference many trusted resources you can find online to help you on your journey.

Be sure to visit www.payingforlongtermcare.com, where you can find the latest information, guides, and free resources to help make your journey smoother and less stressful.

A Common Scenario: Meet Tom—My Stepfather

Most families don't truly understand the complexities of placing a parent or loved one into senior care, and they likely don't want to think about it either! Then crisis hits and they are neither financially nor emotionally prepared for what is about to happen. What's the best place to care for Mom or Dad? How do we pay for it? Where do I search online? Who can I trust? What do we do with the house? What do we do with all the stuff? Many times, siblings are also spread across the United States or even the world, which further compounds the difficulty and stress. It's much more confusing than it should be to understand the scope of options, the levels of care, and how much it will all cost, which leaves families uncertain and overwhelmed. Until now.

You see, this was me too. And it was my family's experience when my stepfather, Tom, became ill and that was part of the inspiration for me to write this book. Tom lived in Louisville, Kentucky, where I grew up, and when he started getting sick, I lived more than 400 miles away in Kansas City. My half-sister, Rebecca, thankfully lived in Louisville and could quarterback things locally. I owe so much to her for being there and stepping up to make sure Tom was always well cared for.

At the time, I was in my forties with two young kids in grade and middle school and in the prime of my career. Then suddenly, or so it seemed, the man I looked up to, who had practically raised me and who loved me unconditionally, was sick—*really* sick. I was worried, a little lost, and sad his life had come to this. The doctors said Tom could no longer live by himself. It was hard to comprehend how his health and independence had declined to this point. It all seemed to happen so fast. Maybe I wasn't paying enough attention, or the 400-mile distance had kept me from seeing the day to day and what was really happening as he aged.

Regardless, it was time for me to pay back the man who had had so much influence over my life and whom I loved just as much as my blood father (Tom and my mother raised me along with my dad in an amazingly healthy co-parenting relationship). He was a wonderful grandpa; he had a big belly, he was jolly and fun, and he loved his grandchildren, Maddy and Charlie. Tom joyfully embraced being a grandpa, proudly parading those kids around to all of his friends, and Tom knew a lot of people. He also had a more interesting life than most of us.

His background included restaurant ownership and training in the thoroughbred industry at Churchill Downs. But possibly his greatest achievement was being an incredibly talented entertainer as a singer for over 50 years. He even had a hit on the Top 10 above Elvis in the 1960s. This is how we all remember Tom: He was such a unique character, and it was so hard for everyone to watch this independent man's health decline and leave him needing help to live a daily life. How many of you can relate to this?

I knew, *or at least I thought I knew*, that he wasn't ready for a nursing home. Not Tom. He would never go for that, and it was depressing to think about him wrapping up such a flamboyant life in a nursing home. There was no way that was going to happen, so we started looking for options that would enable him to stay at home.

I had no idea what I was doing, so Rebecca and I started researching. The research pointed to in-home care, or really, home health care. This seemed simple enough: we could bring someone in so Tom could stay where he was comfortable and be so much happier.

So, we started interviewing home health care companies (or actually Rebecca did because she was local). I had no idea how much home health care cost (or how quickly those costs added up and eroded Tom's savings), but we didn't have a choice. Tom needed care to bathe, eat, move around, and take his medications at the right time; all the basic daily living things those of us who are healthy take for granted, right?

We chose a home health care company and it seemed like things were going well. When I couldn't be there to visit in person, we would talk on the phone daily. It was nice to hear that he had become friends with his caregiver, Sarah (who by the way he thought was kinda cute). Then we noticed he needed more help more often—especially with transferring issues. Tom was a big man, and we had to change caregivers. I'm quite certain that he didn't think the new caregiver Steve was as cute as Sarah!

Once we had things stabilized, we dug in and started planning how to take care of him and pay for care for the rest of Tom's life. I thought this next step would be more straightforward. "This will be easy for me—I'm great with numbers," I said to myself, but boy was I wrong. We were even more unprepared for the "paying for long-term care" part of the process.

Next step, I had to start gathering all of Tom's assets, and I knew this was going to be challenging. Tom was that guy: the guy who would hide money under the mattress (or in the freezer as I found out once accidentally while looking for leftovers). That was Tom—he didn't like banks, and I knew there was little chance he had everything documented in savings accounts, IRAs, or stocks. Could he have a long-term care insurance policy to help with the costs? Not likely, as he wasn't much of a planner, but how could I know for sure? I knew he had some kind of a life insurance policy, but how could I get a copy? It was even more difficult trying to figure this out from 400 miles away, even with Rebecca's help. I was driving eight hours every other weekend to visit Tom and sift through mounds of paper in file cabinets. Tom wasn't much of a technology guy.

I was spending hours digging through records, playing detective to figure out what assets he had to pay for care: cash in the bank and under the mattress, a life insurance policy, home value, vehicles, and anything else I might find to help pay for care. I had discovered there could be a scenario that he could qualify for money from the government, and I needed to be careful, because there are certain assets that could qualify—or more concerning, disqualify—Tom from funding options like veterans benefits or Medicaid. Selling any of his assets might disqualify Tom (and most Americans) from receiving benefits that he had earned over his lifetime, and I didn't want any unintended consequences. (See Chapter 10: Veterans Benefits and Chapter 8: Understanding Medicaid/Medicare.)

After several months of in-home health care, I realized things were much more serious. Tom wasn't getting any better and it became sadly apparent to Rebecca and me that he needed a higher level of care. The guilt set in again: *I am going have to move Tom to assisted living, where he will live out the rest of his life.* It was stressful and the guilt was compounded by not being there every day, but in my mind I had no choice. I had to be there for him. This man had taken care of and guided me so many times, and believe me I was a handful from time to time growing up. I think one of my biggest stressors was that I didn't want to make a mistake. I feared not getting Tom the right care, and I felt the weight of worrying about making a mistake.

I dropped everything and got back to researching options for long-term care. While I didn't think this day would come quite so soon, I knew we had to do something, but what? Where did I start? Who did I call?

I turned to friends, family, and of course the almighty Google search. I'll bet I went to 20 or more sites as I searched long-term care, senior care, nursing homes, and anything else I could think of followed by my city name. Sound familiar? I filled out forms on the sites, asking for information or downloading brochures, anything to help me make the right decision. Then I had to analyze *all* the options. Which one is right? What's the difference between these five care communities besides price? (See Chapter 11: Researching Senior Living Options.)

At this point I was totally overwhelmed and worried about making a mistake, and then as if this wasn't enough to deal with, it happened. My phone started to ring. I was getting calls from care communities—some that I had never even heard of or contacted. How did they get my name? Each one asked a thousand questions—the same questions over and over again—adding an additional layer of stress that we didn't need.

The point of my story? I want you to know it's okay to feel overwhelmed. It's normal to be worried about making mistakes or to be stressed over how you'll pay for long-term care.

Know that you are not alone. I wrote this book for YOU, and to help your family get through this challenging and emotional time. It's natural to feel guilty about all of it—it's one of the most emotional and stressful times you will ever face.

We did get through it and got Tom successfully placed into a care community. And when Tom transitioned into the care community, it allowed me to shift from being a caregiver/administrative assistant/scheduler to being his son. Tom was happy there and lived out the next four months as his health seriously declined. I cherished the fact that I visited Tom as much as possible during that time, because after he passed I had no regrets: I knew I had made every effort to spend as much time with him as I could at the end of his life. During the last few weeks, he lived at home with an in-home hospice nurse where he seemed peaceful, and I was able to have one last hug, cry, and goodbye at his bedside before he passed.

Now, years after Tom passed, I spend 100% of my time in the senior living industry advocating for families to help them in their transition and journey to long-term care. With an in-depth understanding of the process and the industry, shortcuts to find resources, and knowledge on how to pay for care, I want to give back. I hope this resource helps you to not only get through it but also saves you time and stress and helps you access money you may not have realized was available.

I hope my experience helps you learn from my mistakes and is received as a small gift from me to your family. I hope it helps your heart and your mental health and supports you in a positive way during this challenging and stressful time. It's going to be okay—we are here for you. My team and I have built all kinds of free resources to help you and your family to navigate the process, minimize mistakes, and focus on your loved one and the care they need. Let's get started.

Tom and Ben at the
Kentucky State Fair
(1980)

Tom taking the
grandkids, Maddy
and Charlie,
to see the horses

Tom as a jockey agent at Churchill Downs

Tom in the Army Reserves

Tom with his hit band, The Sultans (1959)

PART I

CHAPTER 1

The Facts—70% Will Need Care

None of us has a crystal ball that can tell us whether or not we'll need long-term care in our future. But we do have statistics. Based on research from the U.S. Department of Health and Human Services, an estimated 70% of people over age 65 will require some form of long-term care during their lifetime.

Who's More at Risk?

While anyone has the potential to need long-term care at some point, there are factors that may increase your risk:

- *Age*—Risk increases as you get older
- *Gender*—Women are more likely than men to require long-term care
- *Marital Status*—Single people are more likely to need care
- *Lifestyle*—Poor diet and a lack of exercise can increase risk
- *Health and Family History*—These factors can put you at higher risk

What Is Senior Care?

Senior care, otherwise known as long-term care, is defined by the National Institute on Aging as services designed to meet a person's health or personal care needs. These services can help you live as independently and safely as possible when you can no longer perform everyday activities on your own. This type of care can be provided at home, in an adult day care, in a senior living community, or through skilled nursing.

The Cost of Senior Care

Fidelity reports that a 65-year-old couple retiring in 2019 could expect to spend $285,000 on long-term care costs during retirement. More on this later.

Sometimes It's Sudden

The need for senior care can develop gradually as a person ages and/or as an illness or disability worsens. All too often the need for senior care arises suddenly, as a result of a fall, heart attack, or stroke.

The Benefits of Planning Ahead

Rather than gamble on being part of the lucky 30% that won't need care or on being able to recognize that the need is coming in time to prepare, it's crucial to plan for "what ifs" to gain these benefits:

- You'll have time to truly think through your needs and wants to find the best fit.
- You can carefully research ALL your options without pressure.

- You're taking control of the future rather than letting reaction drive decisions.
- By having more ownership in the process, you'll feel more confident about your decision.
- Your family will be less stressed with a plan.

CHAPTER 2

It's OK to Be Stressed

Even though we know aging is a normal part of life, it doesn't make it any less difficult, especially when it's your loved one or parent. It can feel surreal when the roles reverse and you shift from child to caregiver and/or decision maker. However, not only are you and your family dealing with the emotions of the adjustment, you're also faced with the responsibility of ensuring that your loved one or parent gets the best care. You want to do the right thing for them, *but what exactly is that?* Enter the stress.

Key Stressors

Honoring Their Wishes

The reality is that while more than 90% of Americans believe it is important to discuss their care wishes, only 32% have actually had these conversations, according to The Conversation Project's 2018 National Survey. If your loved one or parent can no longer share their wishes, it's heartbreaking and most certainly makes decisions more complicated. Note: Be sure to have these important conversations about your future sooner rather than later.

Fear of Making a Mistake

From identifying options to researching them to choosing the best one, it seems like there are so many opportunities for error! And again, is this what my loved one or parent would truly want? You may never know for sure, but that doesn't mean you can't make an informed decision. Analysis paralysis (when a decision is unable to be made due to overthinking) happens far too often, and the result is that the senior doesn't get the care they need, or get it soon enough to be as beneficial as it could be.

Guilt

According to Marilyn A Mendoza, Ph.D., a clinical instructor in the psychiatry department at Tulane University Medical Center and a psychologist specializing in bereavement, "Guilt is a part of caregiving, particularly when you have to make a decision that you know is against the wishes of your loved one." All that we can do is our best, and we simply cannot do it all. It's normal to feel overly responsible and helpless at the same time. Despite our best intentions and efforts, feeling guilty is part of the process of making decisions for an aging loved one.

But the guilt that most of us feel is unjustified. Sometimes doing what's best for a loved one means that the responsibilities and decisions we're faced with are not what anyone would have wanted. There can be countless other emotions involved with transitioning a loved one into a care community, including worry, anger, anxiety, and resentment.

Mendoza offers the following suggestions for emotionally processing these decisions:

- Acknowledge that you feel guilty and accept that feeling guilt is a normal part of caregiving.

- Recognize that you are only human and not a superhero who's capable of doing everything.
- Avoid making promises to your loved one that you aren't practical or possible.
- Be kind to yourself and take care of your own needs.
- Talk to friends and family and write down any thoughts or feelings.
- Have a conversation with your loved one as if they're in front of you. Tell them that you're struggling with guilt, then imagine what they would say in response. The vast majority of our loved ones do not want us to be in pain or distress.
- If you cannot reconcile with your guilt, seek out a mental health professional. It's both physically and emotionally unhealthy to carry these types of emotions around.
- Forgive yourself. You are doing your best.

Figuring Out Finances

Financial decisions of this magnitude are stressful in any situation, but when looking at senior care, this is compounded by the confusion around pricing for different levels of care, payment structures, add-on services, and what options, if any, can help offset the cost (we'll get to this later). What's more, so many families have to chase down assets, life insurance, and/or long-term care policies and debts and determine what to do with the house and the stuff; it's overwhelming. I've been there! Again, note: Have these details organized for your loved ones so they don't suffer the burden.

The modern reality for seniors is that the distance between being healthy today and not tomorrow is shorter than you may realize. According to a 2009 report prepared by the American Health Care

Association and the National Center for Assisted Living, residents spend an average of 28 months in an assisted living facility (the median is 21 months).

> The reason I share this with you is that you may be stressing and thinking that you have to pay for care for 10 years. But depending on where you are in your family's journey, this is statistically unlikely if your loved one is moving to assisted living. You very likely are planning to pay for 2-3 years. Think about this as you plan and select the care community.

Common Aging Fears

Remember that your loved one or parent is likely struggling with this transition too.

Common fears for seniors include:

- Loss of independence
- Loss of mental acuity
- Declining health
- Running out of money
- Needing to leave their home
- Losing loved ones
- Becoming dependent on others
- Not being able to drive
- Social isolation and loneliness
- Falling or becoming incapacitated

By understanding their fears and showing empathy, your loved one will be comforted in knowing that you're on their side. While the best support is to listen, make sure you also involve them as much as possible by asking how you can help instead of making decisions for them. Remember, no one wants to be told that we "have to" do something we don't want, especially if we weren't included in that decision.

If the Stress Becomes Too Much

While stress during this time is normal, if it gets in the way of your daily activities for several days in a row, you should call your healthcare provider. You should never feel uncomfortable about asking for help. You should give yourself a break—it's okay to be stressed! These feelings are real, valid, and common. Allow yourself time to process and grieve the change, but at the same time take heart that you're doing your best. That's all anyone can ask. Many of us have been through this. You are not alone.

CHAPTER 3

Understanding Senior Service Providers and Resources

At first glance, the senior care industry can almost feel like the old Abbott and Costello bit, "Who's on First?" You don't know who the players are or what they can help with. In this case, though, it's frustrating and stressful instead of humorous. To help, here's a big picture look at the senior care industry and its stakeholders.

Navigating Care and Service Needs

Geriatric Care Managers—These are (generally) licensed nurses or social workers who specialize in geriatrics. You can think of them as private advocates and guides who can help you and your family to identify and meet your needs.

Placement Agents—These are professionals who help families determine which local senior living communities would be best suited for their loved ones. They understand the landscape of the local market and have relationships with care communities. By spending time with you and your family to understand the senior's needs, they can evaluate the best match between your loved one and the right community. Their services are provided to families free of charge.

Care Coordinators—Think of them as the liaison for seniors and families in a care network focused on addressing the needs of the senior. They supervise interdisciplinary care by bringing together the different specialists whose help the patient may need. The coordinator is also responsible for monitoring and evaluating the care delivered. They can answer questions and perform assessments.

Benefits

VA Accredited Representatives—Individuals who have undergone a formal application and training process and are recognized by the U.S. Department of Veterans Affairs (VA) as being capable of assisting claimants. (See Chapter 10: Veterans Benefits.)

Certified Medicaid Planners (CMPs) —These are professionals in the Medicaid planning field who have been certified by the Certified Medicaid Planning Governing Board. They can help you navigate through the current rules of Medicaid and find the most cost-effective plan for your situation. (See Chapter 8: Understanding Medicare/Medicaid.)

Legal

Elder Law Attorneys—They handle a wide range of legal issues affecting a senior or disabled person, including issues related to health care, long-term care planning, guardianship, retirement, Social Security, Medicare/Medicaid, and other important matters. (See Chapter 4: Elder Law Attorneys.)

Real Estate

Realtors—These are real estate agents who can help you to list your house for sale in a traditional way. They typically work on commission and are paid a percentage of the property's sale price. (See Chapter 10: Selling the Family Home.)

"As-Is" Certified Home Buyers—These are not realtors, but individuals who specialize in purchasing homes for cash in "as-is" condition with all the "stuff." They do not charge a commission for their services. (See Chapter 10: Selling the Family Home.)

Financial Planning

Financial Planners—Offer services that address the unique and evolving financial, demographic, health, and emotional needs of seniors and their evolving needs. (See Chapter 10: Funding Strategies to Pay for Immediate Needs.)

Tax Planners—These professionals have a keen understanding of the operational, compliance, and strategic planning issues and are a great resource for senior care planning.

Insurance Brokers/Agents—They offer services such as long-term care insurance, long-term care riders, life insurance conversions, and annuities, any of which could be used to help pay for senior care.

Lenders—Help with short-term loans known as bridge loans can be used until a senior secures permanent financing or removes an existing obligation. Bridge loans are up to one year, have a little higher interest rate, and may be unsecured or backed by some form of collateral, such as real estate.

Reverse Mortgage Brokers—They issue a mortgage loan, usually secured by a residential property, that enables the senior to access the equity of the property. (See Chapter 10: Reverse Mortgages.)

Additional Support and Care Providers

Social Workers—These professionals collaborate with patients, their families, and their care team to promote physical and mental well-being following an illness, hospitalization, or other medical event.

Private Duty Nurses—Registered nurses (RN) or licensed practical nurses (LPN/LVN) who works one-on-one with individual patients and/or their families. Many provide their services at the homes of their patients.

Hospital Discharge Workers—These individuals help coordinate the information and care you'll need after you leave the hospital.

Home Health Care Agency—They connect families with pre-screened caregivers that match the care needs of your loved one or parent.

Downsizing Experts—Estate sale companies and specialists who can offer resources and tips and help you deal with all the 'stuff' as you prepare to sell a home.

CHAPTER 4

Elder Law Attorneys

Elder law attorneys can help families preserve their assets as they pay for long-term care. These specialized attorneys not only have a deeper understanding of real-life issues involving the aging process, but they're also tied to a large network of other elder care professionals who could be helpful to you and your family. Along with helping your family to navigate long-term care options, an elder law attorney can help your family maintain financial autonomy through proper financial and legal planning.

Elder law encompasses a wide range of legal fields, all of which specifically advocate for seniors and their families. Some of these fields include:

- Administration and Management of Estates and Trusts
- Conservatorship and Guardianship
- Elder Abuse and Fraud
- Estate Planning, including:
  - Wills and Trusts
  - Durable Powers of Attorney

- Long-Term Care Placement in Assisted Living Communities
- Medicaid Benefits
- Medicare Appeals and Claims
- Probate
- Supplemental and Long-Term Care Insurance Issues
- Veterans Benefits

Keep in Mind

Most elder law attorneys will not specialize in every single one of these areas, so it's important to retain an attorney who has experience with addressing your family's specific needs.

CHAPTER RESOURCES

- To find an elder law attorney in your area, visit www.payingforlongtermcare.com/ela

CHAPTER 5

Overview of Senior Living Options

If your loved one or parent has come to the point where they need senior care, or will soon, it's important to understand all of the options available. It's also important to understand that no senior living option is designed to be "one size fits all."

There are currently numerous different levels of care available in multiple different settings that have been designed to best suit the individual needs of your loved one. This is not "one-stop shopping;" typically, care arrangements work for a definitive period of time. But as your loved one's needs change, so will their care and services (and the costs of these).

Types of Communities

Senior Care at Home

The types of care offered at home include:

Home Care – Includes professional support services that allow a person to live safely in their home. Home care can involve companionship, help with daily activities such as bathing and dressing, safely managing tasks around the house, etc.

Home Health Care—This is typically physician-directed care intended to help patients prevent or recover from injuries, illnesses, or hospital stays. Provides assistance with activities of daily living.

Personal Care and Companionship—Provides assistance with activities of daily living (ADLs) such as bathing, dressing, and mobility. Companion care provides companionship and non-medical services such as meal preparation and light household chores.

Private Duty Nursing Care—Provides long-term, hourly nursing care for those with chronic illnesses, injuries, or disabilities.

Adult Day Care—This option offers your loved one or parent a safe, stimulating social environment in a professional care setting during normal business hours, five days a week. Some services may be available in the evenings or on weekends. Although services vary, you can typically expect:

- Meals and snacks, health monitoring, medication assistance, and fitness, as well as enrichment programs and social activities

Some adult day care centers also offer personal care services, such as bathing or nail care.

Care in Senior Living

Senior living offers a range of different levels of care, which include:

Senior Rehabilitation Centers—These are in-patient facilities that provide therapy and treatment designed to restore functioning and reduce pain after an injury or serious medical event. Senior rehab centers are often used in the transition between hospital and home or long-term care.

Rehab facilities typically include services such as:

- *Physical therapy* to improve balance and mobility, manage pain, and increase strength
- *Occupational therapy* to help with activities of daily living
- *Speech therapy* to assist with conditions affecting communication or cognitive skills, such as memory problems

Your loved one's health will dictate whether they need short-term or long-term rehabilitation. Generally, your loved one may only require a short stay in a rehab facility after a minor surgery. However, more chronic, serious conditions may require several months of rehab services at a skilled nursing facility that offers around-the-clock care.

Respite Care—Provides temporary institutional care for seniors who are dependent, elderly, ill, or handicapped. Respite care is typically used for a short period of time to provide care and rest for both the senior as well as the caregiver(s). This type of care can be provided in a senior's home as well as in a care facility.

Independent Living—This refers to any housing arrangement designed exclusively for older adults. The types of housing vary widely, from apartment-style living to single-family homes. Housing is generally designed to be more accommodating to aging adults and is often more compact and easier to navigate, with little maintenance or yard work to worry about.

This level of care is designed for seniors who need or want assistance with Instrumental Activities of Daily Living (IADLs). IADLs require more complex planning and thinking than the basic self-care tasks of Activities of Daily Living (ADLs). Examples of IADLs include managing a budget, paying bills, preparing meals, arranging medical appointments, and completing housework. In other words, the basic essential functions of survival are not threatened. However, they are seeking more social and enrichment opportunities than they would have at home, as well as freedom from the hassle of chores and household maintenance.

You can typically expect:

- A choice of accommodations such as apartments, condominiums, and/or free-standing villas or cottages as well as a range of floorplan options
- Worry-free living with housekeeping, laundry, and home maintenance taken care of, as well as restaurant-style dining and transportation services
- Plenty of social opportunities, activities, and clubs
- Amenities such as concierge services, a pool, fitness center, library, and onsite salon

Keep in mind that onsite medical care is typically not offered in independent living. If assistance with ADLs is needed, or there are serious health issues to address, a third-party service or higher level of care would be necessary.

Assisted Living—This level of care is designed for seniors who need assistance with ADLs, or basic self-care tasks, including but not limited to eating, bathing, and dressing. In addition to housing, amenities, and enrichment opportunities, this level of care also provides onsite care and support while encouraging the independence of residents.

There are typically 20 to 120 rooms for residents and more apartment-style than the smaller residential assisted living facilities. Many of the larger senior living communities are part of a local, regional, or national brand and offer different levels of services and amenities. Pricing and contracts vary greatly depending on location, level of care, and payment type.

You can typically expect:

- Individualized support with bathing, dressing, eating, and medication as well as onsite medical care.
- A comfortable, homelike setting without the worry of home upkeep, cooking, cleaning, and yard maintenance
- Features that include spacious accommodations, 24-hour supervision, and a secure environment as well as scheduled transportation
- Amenities such as fitness centers, libraries, and onsite salons
- Daily social opportunities with a range of scheduled programs, activities, and outings
- Specialized care services for those with incontinence or chronic health issues

Residential Assisted Living

Another consideration is a smaller assisted living community. Residential assisted living communities are smaller buildings and range from six to 20 residents. These buildings are usually nestled into a suburban neighborhood and have more of an intimate, home-like feel.

Memory Care—This level of care is designed to exclusively support and nurture those with Alzheimer's disease and other forms of dementia. It's estimated that over 80% of individuals in assisted living for the physically frail have moderate to severe dementia. Many residents have other forms of memory loss, such as substance abusers, individuals with later stages of Parkinson's disease, etc. Memory Care is a secure environment, designed for residents who are considered at risk of wandering or elopement.

You can typically expect:

- Staff training that includes a deeper understanding of dementia, care needs, and techniques for managing challenging behaviors
- 24-hour supervision in a secure environment with emergency call systems and layouts that are easy to navigate
- Therapy activities based on cognitive abilities and programs with social opportunities
- Accommodations that include private or semi-private rooms as well as housekeeping, laundry, and supportive dining

Memory care is similar to assisted living but provides special care and support for those with progressive memory impairment. Memory care units will generally feature enhanced security features—which may include tracking bracelets and secure outside areas—to prevent residents from wandering.

It's also common to find calming colors, larger windows for more natural light, cozy gathering spaces, and programs tailored to reduce anxiety in residents, which is commonly associated with dementia.

Senior Care in Skilled Nursing

This is the highest level of care and what you would typically consider a nursing home. Skilled nursing is designed for those with chronic health conditions or incontinence, who require dispensing and monitoring intravenous medications and/or who are recovering after a surgery or hospitalization. Assisted living and skilled nursing facilities are licensed by the state in which they are located.

Many skilled nursing facilities offer 24-hour supervised care with a visiting physician and licensed staff on site in addition to physical, speech, and occupational therapists, social workers, psychologists and others.

You can typically expect:

- Private or semi-private rooms in an environment that feels more like a hospital setting
- Assistance with daily living, health monitoring, and medication management
- Exercise programs, social opportunities, and activities
- Services such as housekeeping, laundry service, and meals
- They may specialize in short-term or acute nursing care,

intermediate care, or long-term skilled nursing care. All staff members have passed background checks and are trained to work with this frail population.

The Advantages of All-In-One

You may not realize that while some senior living communities stand alone as independent living, assisted living, or memory care, others offer the full continuum of care all on one campus. This can benefit your loved one or parent in several ways:

- They don't have to move from place to place as their health needs evolve.
- They are able to stay with friends and in the comfort of familiar surroundings.
- They will have continuity in care, which provides added peace of mind.

Other Types of Facilities

The range of housing options and the varying levels of care offered within senior communities help ensure that every senior will find a perfect match for their housing needs and lifestyle.

55+ Active Adult Communities

Independent living apartments are ideal for seniors who do not need personal or medical care but who would like to live with other seniors who share similar interests. In most independent living facilities seniors can take advantage of planned community events, field trips, shopping excursions, and on-premise projects. These apartments are not licensed or regulated.

Adult Homes

Adult homes are licensed and regulated for temporary or long-term residence by adults unable to live independently. They usually include supervision, personal care, housekeeping, and three meals a day.

Family-Type Homes

Family-type homes, also called group homes, board homes, and care homes, offer long-term residential care, housekeeping, and supervision for four or fewer adults unrelated to the operator. The department of Social Services oversees their operations.

Continuing Care Retirement Communities

Continuing care retirement communities, also known as life care or life plan communities, offer a variety of facilities, from assisted living to skilled nursing, all on one campus. They provide independent living, assisted living, memory care, and/or skilled nursing on one campus. They facilitate "aging in place"; that is, the resident can move from one level of care to the next as their needs change. The transition to skilled nursing is easier for residents, because they are able to remain in familiar surroundings. They may require a "buy-in", or an up-front entry fee followed by monthly payments that cover services, amenities, and needed medical care. There are different types of contracts designed around level of care costs and payment included for a specified number of days of care.

Payment Structures

Most senior living options are rental communities with an annual or month-to-month contract (which can be dictated by state licensing). Rental communities require a community fee (typically less than or equal to one month's fee) and a monthly fee plus care fees. Most continuing care retirement communities are buy-in and require an entry fee and monthly fee for services. Care costs in assisted living facilities can be packages or levels of care, "boutique," or "à la carte" to pay for individual services, or all inclusive (rent and care).

Don't let all of these options overwhelm you! There are professionals who specialize in helping families find the community that's right for their loved one.

CHAPTER RESOURCES

- Find a list of senior care professionals in your area who can help with evaluating your loved one's needs at www.payingforlongtermcare.com/pro

CHAPTER 6

Staying at Home vs. Moving into a Senior Community

Now that you have a better understanding of the options for your loved one or parent as well as the costs, you may think that in-home care is the best option. Honestly, you've probably thought this since the beginning, right? Most people do! In fact, nearly 90% of people over age 65 want to stay at home for as long as possible according to the American Association of Retired Persons (AARP). It's difficult to imagine your loved one needing to leave their home and they likely don't want to either. It's *home*, where your family has made so many memories, where your loved one or parent is most comfortable, and where you may feel they belong. But emotions aside, there are a number of factors to consider in determining whether home truly is the best option. What's more, you may be surprised that staying home is *not* always less expensive than transitioning to a care community.

The TOTAL Cost of Staying Home

It may seem that staying at home would cost less. But, if you're basing that on the cost of home care plus your mortgage or rent, it's not necessarily an apples-to-apples comparison. Don't forget that your other monthly out-of-pocket expenses at home include food, utilities, cable, internet, home and yard maintenance, property taxes, and entertainment costs. This is the TOTAL cost of living at home and it's imperative to factor everything in. All of these expenses are typically included in the monthly cost of care communities.

You may also have to arrange for accessibility modifications at home, which can be an expensive hassle. Installing wheelchair ramps, for example, can cost $1,000 to as much as $15,000, and widening a doorway can range from $500 to $1,000 (if there are no structural issues!).

Lastly, be sure to budget for those unexpected expenses that come with home ownership—particularly if your loved one or parent's house is older—like replacing the HVAC, roof, and hot water heater and other maintenance costs.

After you consider these factors, a care community could actually cost less than staying at home.

Quality of Life Considerations

When making a decision between staying at home and transitioning to a care community, it goes without saying that quality of life should be the biggest consideration. If your loved one or parent will be living with you or with a spouse, or has a strong support network, staying home may very well be the best option right now. But quality of life is a dynamic concept that means different things to different people.

Oftentimes—especially if they live alone and/or their families live far away—the senior is isolated at home and may suffer cognitive decline more rapidly. It's common to see a shrinking social circle for the senior as the result of staying at home. A community almost always provides seniors with greater opportunities for social interaction.

Be sure to take the following considerations to heart.

Falls

Your loved one's safety must always be a top priority. The Centers for Disease Control and Prevention (CDC) reports that nearly a third of seniors fall each year and about half of all the falls requiring hospitalization occur at home. Help reduce the risk of a fall by taking some of the following precautions around your loved one's home:

- Clear all walking paths of clutter
- Ensure that every room has adequate lighting
- Remove all throw rugs
- Install grab bars and non-slip mats in the bathroom

Fire Prevention

An average of over 7,000 people age 65 and older die each year in the United States due to a home injury. While falls are the leading cause, fires are second, according to the Home Safety Council (HSC). To help prevent them, your loved one or parent should stay in the kitchen when cooking, disconnect the stove and use only the microwave, avoid wearing loose-fitting clothing, and keep flammable items away from the cooktop. They should also avoid space heaters, or keep them three feet or more from flammable items and turn them off when leaving the room. Be sure to inspect their furnace and/or fireplace annually and make sure that electrical outlets or extension cords are never overloaded. Ensure that all smoke detectors have new batteries at least twice a year, but never allow the senior to change these batteries, as this poses a significant fall risk.

Medication

A National Institutes of Health study found that 40% of seniors take five or more prescriptions, yet as many as 55% take these medications incorrectly. To reduce the potential for error, make sure your loved one or parent always follows the instructions exactly, that they read the package insert fully, and that they take medications for the full duration even if they feel better. It's also helpful to keep track of medications as well as dosage times with pill organizers or even apps where you can set reminders. (See Chapter 14: How Technology Can Help with Companionship and Safety.)

Social Isolation

Of all you worry about when it comes to your parent or loved one, their social life may not be high on the list. But it should be. Social isolation—defined as a near-total or complete lack of contact between an individual and society—has been called a growing health epidemic among seniors by the AARP Foundation. Multiple studies have shown a direct link between social isolation and poor health; social isolation is associated with a roughly 50% increased risk of dementia and a substantially increased risk of premature death from all causes. One study found that the health risks of prolonged isolation were equivalent to the dangers of smoking 15 cigarettes a day. Living alone is one of the biggest risk factors for social isolation and loneliness. If your parent or loved one lives alone, it's important to develop a plan with friends and family for maintaining daily communication and contact.

Nutrition

Proper nutrition is absolutely crucial for seniors, but it can be complicated. Your loved one may need increased amounts of certain nutrients, they may have slower metabolism, their palate and digestion may change, and chronic conditions or medications may require dietary restrictions. This could explain why senior malnutrition costs the United States $51.3 billion a year, according to the Alliance on Aging Research. For help, check out the National Institute on Aging's (NIA) website. Their Healthy Eating section offers resources such as information on healthy food shopping on a budget, nutrition requirements for seniors, and even sample menus and shopping lists. If it's difficult for your loved one to shop and prepare meals each day, meal delivery is another option.

Fitness

Known as the sitting disease, a sedentary lifestyle can put your loved one or parent at greater risk for conditions such as high blood pressure, stroke, cardiovascular disease, some cancers, Type 2 diabetes, and even cognitive decline. And it's more common than you may think. A U.S. National Health and Nutrition Examination Survey found that 67% of adults aged 60 and older are sedentary for at least 8.5 hours a day. To help your loved one or parent stay active at home, the NIA recommends that seniors do at least 150 minutes of moderate-intensity physical activity throughout the week in sessions of at least 10 minutes duration across four categories of exercise: endurance, strength training, balance, and flexibility.

Driving

According to the American Automobile Association (AAA), some of the biggest risks for senior drivers are that weaker muscles and limited range of motion can restrict their ability to grip/turn the steering wheel, press the accelerator or brake, or open doors and windows. If your loved one or parent still needs to drive while at home, make sure to keep up with regular checkups, particularly for vision and hearing, so you can manage any issues that affect driving before they become a danger.

Sometimes Illness Can be Easy to Overlook

When you live with another person, they may notice signs and symptoms of illness that you don't on your own. But, if your loved one or parent is one of the over 11 million seniors living alone per the Administration on Aging, illness can be easy to miss. Take Alzheimer's disease for example. According to the Alzheimer's Association someone in the United States develops it every 65 seconds, and one in 10 people age 65 and older has it. But early symptoms can be hard to spot and may be more obvious to other people than to your loved one or parent themselves.

If you live long distance, it's time to visit mom/dad in their home for a few hours to observe them and their environment and have a meal with them.

- Has there been a change in their housekeeping (once fastidious, now very lax)?
- Take note of their hygiene. Are there stains on their clothes? Is their hair unkempt?
- Has there been a change in their attitude or demeanor?
- Watch them navigate their environment. Has their gait changed? Are they having balance issues and needing to hold onto things in order to move around?
- Look in their bedroom, bathroom, refrigerator, pantry/cabinets. Is there food? Are there expired medications?
- Are there indications of accidents on carpets or in bathrooms?

Emergency Preparedness

The importance of being prepared for emergencies applies to everyone. But special precautions should be taken if an aging loved one is staying at home. Keep poison control as well as neighbor phone numbers handy for them. Also, identify (and make sure they've practiced) two ways to exit in an emergency. Place smoke alarms and carbon monoxide detectors on each floor or near each bedroom and check them twice a year. Note that the senior should *not* be responsible for doing this, since ladders present a major risk for falling. Fire extinguishers should be easily accessible, and if your loved one has mobility issues, you might consider a home fire sprinkler system. In addition, consider purchasing a backup generator if they use oxygen equipment and/or a dialysis machine. They should also have a personal emergency response system (wearable call button or in-home voice-activated system) on at all times. (See Chapter 14: How Technology Can Help with Companionship and Safety for more ideas.)

Senior Care Communities Cover Quality of Life Considerations

It's understandable if all of this seems overwhelming to manage. Keep in mind that care communities are designed specifically with these considerations as standard practice. Knowing that your loved ones are in a safe and healthy environment removes a tremendous amount of burden and worry.

Communities focus on the overall well-being of residents and offer a worry-free lifestyle with amenities and social opportunities. These are concepts that are quite simply difficult to replicate at home. Having care available 24/7 also offers considerable peace of mind.

CHAPTER RESOURCES

- Visit www.payingforlongtermcare.com/calc to calculate the costs of living at home vs. in a care community
- Complete a senior safety walk-through of the home with a printable checklist from www.payingforlongtermcare.com/safety
- Visit www.payforlongtermcare.com/signs for expanded resources to recognize the warning signs that your aging loved one may no longer be able to live independently
- Find in-home care services in your area at www.payingforlongtermcare.com/home

CHAPTER 7

The Cost of Long-Term Care

The U.S. Census indicates that 10,000 Baby Boomers will turn 65 every day from now until 2030, and, as noted in Chapter 1, the vast majority will need long-term care at some point. Most families are blindsided by the astronomical costs of care and often panic about how they'll pay for it. I've been there myself. Knowing the cost is a first step to helping you plan for care. To help your family prepare, here are the median annual costs by level of care and type of setting according to the 2020 Genworth Cost of Care Survey:

Care at Home

- Home Health Care
    - Home Care Homemaker Services —$53,768
    - Home Care Home Health Aide Services —$54,912

Care in Senior Living

- Community and Assisted Living
    - Adult Day Health Care—$19,240
    - Assisted Living Facility—$51,600
    - Semi-Private Room Nursing Home—$93,075
    - Private Room Nursing Home—$105,850

There's a wide range of costs for care across the United States. Find the 2020 average costs of long-term care in your state at www.payingforlongtermcare.com/costs.

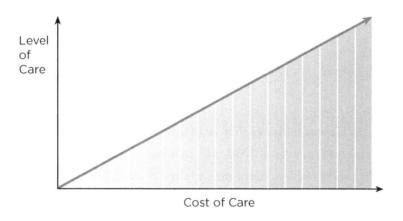

What Affects the Cost of Long-Term Care?

Costs could be higher or lower for your family based on a variety of factors, but there are three main drivers that affect what you'll pay: level of care, geography, and amenities. The good thing is these factors do give you some control over what you'll pay. Here's how:

1. Level of Care—The higher the level of care your loved one needs, the higher the cost you'll pay for senior living. This is one of the many reasons it's helpful to plan ahead: You can search for communities that offer a full continuum of care on the same campus. If your loved one doesn't currently need daily assistance but would benefit from, for example, having meals prepared or housekeeping taken care of, they

could start in independent living and pay less now. If your loved one needs higher levels of care later on, transitioning to it would be much easier in familiar surroundings and with continuity of care.

2. Geography—As with costs of living, costs of care are also affected by location. For example, here's how annual costs can vary in assisted living alone according to Genworth's 2020 Costs of Long-Term Care by State report:

- 12 months of care in a private, one-bedroom Assisted Living Facility in Delaware averages $80,280, while in Missouri it averages $36,000

To bring your monthly costs down for senior living or skilled nursing, you might consider communities outside the city, in nearby towns, or even in a different state if feasible.

3. Amenities—This is an area where you have the most control. Amenities are typically add-ons to standard monthly costs, and conveniences come at a cost, so it's up to you whether they make sense for your budget.

Common add-ons in senior living include:

- Size of living space—Perhaps a studio or one-bedroom would work for your loved one instead of a two-bedroom.
- Pet fees—There are typically additional fees to bring pets into a community (although the companionship may very well be worth every penny).
- Concierge services—This is most common in independent living and, while certainly convenient, you could

instead have family and/or friends help with shopping or errands, house sitting, and/or pet services if your loved one needs it.
- Private transportation—It's far more convenient to go where you need when you want, but most senior living communities have scheduled transportation for shopping and errands included in the standard monthly cost. Private transportation is offered free or for a nominal fee by most communities.

CHAPTER RESOURCES

- Find the 2020 average costs of senior care in your state at www.payingforlongtermcare.com/costs

CHAPTER 8

Understanding Medicare and Medicaid

Many families assume that Medicare and/or Medicaid will cover the costs of their loved one's long-term care. Others believe that Medicare supplement (Medigap) insurance covers the long-term care services not reimbursed by Medicare. Unfortunately, that's not entirely true. Here's a breakdown of what is covered.

Medicare

Medicare is a federal healthcare benefits program that was designed to help pay for medical expenses of seniors age 65 and older. Mostly covering hospital and physician services, Medicare does offer some limited benefits for assisted living care and home health care. Medicare beneficiaries can choose between the Original Medicare plan (which operates on a fee-for-service basis) or a Medicare Advantage Plan (a private-sector plan, previously called Part C, that can cover extra services not covered by Original Medicare).

- Medicare Part A (hospital insurance) helps pay for inpatient care in a hospital or limited time at a skilled nursing facility (following a hospital stay). Part A will also pay for some in-home health care and hospice care.

- Medicare Part B (medical insurance) helps pay for services from doctors and other health care providers, outpatient care, home health care, durable medical equipment, and some preventive services.
- Supplemental (Medigap) policies help pay Medicare out-of-pocket copayment, coinsurance, and deductible expenses.
- Medicare Part D (Medicare prescription drug coverage) helps cover the cost of prescription drugs.

Regardless of whether they choose Original Medicare or Medicare Advantage, everyone enrolled in Medicare is entitled to the same basic benefits. These benefits include coverage for:

- Medically necessary services to diagnose and treat illnesses
- Medical equipment and devices that your physician has deemed necessary (including wheelchairs, prosthetics, and oxygen)
- Preventative care services and routine physical exams

Medicare only pays for long-term care if you require skilled services or rehabilitative care:

- In a nursing home for a maximum of 100 days; however, the average Medicare-covered stay is much shorter (22 days).
- At home if you are also receiving skilled home health or other in-home services. Generally, long-term care services are covered for only for a short period of time.

It's important to note that Medicare helps with the cost of healthcare, but it does not cover all medical expenses or the cost of most long-term care services. For example, it doesn't pay for non-skilled assistance with Activities of Daily Living (ADL), which make up the majority of long-term care services.

Keep in Mind

- Some people will automatically receive Medicare benefits and others will need to sign up. You may need to sign up if you're 65 (or nearly 65) and not receiving Social Security.
- There are certain times of the year when you can sign up or change how you get coverage.
- You can avoid a penalty by signing up for Medicare Part B when you're first eligible.
- You can choose how you get your Medicare coverage: If you choose to have Original Medicare (Part A and Part B) coverage, you can purchase a Medicare Supplement Insurance (Medigap) policy from a private insurance company.

How to Apply for Medicare

Social Security automatically enrolls you in Original Medicare (Part A and Part B).

Most people age 65 or older are eligible for free Medical hospital insurance (Part A) if they have worked and paid Medicare taxes over the course of their lives. You can enroll in Medicare medical insurance (Part B) by paying a monthly premium.

If you're eligible at age 65, your initial enrollment period begins three months before your 65th birthday, includes the month you turn age 65, and ends three months after your birthday.

If you decide not to enroll in Medicare Part B and then choose to do so later, you may have to pay a higher monthly premium for as long as you have Part B. Your monthly premium may go up 10% for each 12-month period you were eligible for Part B but didn't sign up for it. If you don't enroll in Medicare Part B during your initial enrollment period, you'll have another chance each year to sign up during a general enrollment period that extends from January 1 through March 31. Your coverage begins on July 1 of the year you enroll. You won't need to sign up for Medicare each year, but you will have a chance each year to review your coverage and change plans.

Medicaid

Jointly funded by the federal government and state governments, Medicaid is currently the single largest payer of long-term care expenses in the United States. Unlike Medicare, Medicaid offers extensive benefits for long-term care, but only for those who are considered impoverished. Some people who would not be considered poor when they first needed long-term care are eventually able to rely on Medicaid after they've spent nearly all of their assets and income on services. This is a process called "spending down," and while it can help to meet senior care needs, there are significant drawbacks.

Benefit provisions vary from state to state, but federal guidelines require all states to provide a minimal benefit package, including hospital inpatient and outpatient care, physician care, and other services. All states are required to pay for nursing home care, and they must also pay for home health care for those who would need nursing home care if they did not receive home care. An increasing number of states also pay benefits for home and community-based services, including personal care, home health services, rehabilitation, therapy, adult day care, homemaker services, and other services. A few states will also pay for long-term care services received in an assisted living community.

Unlike Medicare, with its highly restrictive conditions for payment of nursing home or home care benefits, Medicaid generally meets the need for long-term care for those who qualify. But there are important limitations to Medicaid's long-term care benefits.

Medicaid coverage of home and community-based services is expanding but still fairly limited, and not all states extend coverage beyond the federally required home care for seniors who are nursing home eligible.

While a few states offer benefits for care in an assisted living community, they generally pay only for long-term care services (such as assistance with ADLs), not for room and board. Medicaid covers nursing home care only if it is provided in a Medicaid-certified facility. Most nursing homes are Medicaid-certified, but not all.

Keep in Mind

For those below a certain income level, Medicaid is usually the only way to meet long-term care needs. Those who are not poor but are considering spending down in order to obtain Medicaid benefits should be aware of several disadvantages to this approach.

Spending down generally leaves a person with extremely limited assets and income and results in the loss of financial independence. An elderly person who has worked hard and been self-supporting their whole life must then rely on the government for their needs. Spending down also means that hard-earned assets cannot be used for such purposes as helping grandchildren afford college, and they cannot be left to heirs.

In addition, the types of long-term care available to a Medicaid recipient are often limited. Benefits for home and community-based services are not offered everywhere, eligibility for them may be restricted, and funding is generally limited. And only a few state programs pay benefits for care in assisted living residences. Consequently, some seniors who could be cared for at home are forced to transition to a nursing home.

Finally, a Medicaid recipient may have a more limited choice of long-term care facilities, and the facilities considered the most desirable may not be available. High-quality assisted living communities can easily fill their beds with higher-paying non-Medicaid patients, so they generally won't accept Medicaid recipients. Nursing homes that do admit Medicaid patients sometimes assign only a limited number of beds to them, and the most popular communities often have long waiting lists for Medicaid recipients.

Consequently, Medicaid recipients often end up in facilities that, although certified by Medicaid and considered adequate, are found by some to be less desirable for various reasons. Another consideration is that, if fewer facilities are open to a Medicaid recipient, a senior may have to go wherever beds are available, which could be a distance from family and friends.

To summarize, those who rely on Medicaid to meet their long-term care needs could lose their assets and financial independence, and they often have limited choices of types of care and facilities.

How to Apply for Medicaid

Even though Medicaid is a joint federal and state program, each state operates the administrative aspects of the program, which includes receiving applications and determining eligibility. In order to apply for Medicaid, you must contact the local office in your state. You can apply for Medicaid yourself, or you can designate another person to apply for you (such as a family member or an elder law attorney). Some states will require a face-to-face interview.

To apply for Medicaid you will need to:

- Fill out an application form
- Provide documentation to verify general and financial requirements

If your state finds you eligible for Medicaid, you'll need to go through a functional eligibility assessment to receive long-term care services.

If you own a home, your state might ask you to document the current fair market value of the home and any loans for the home, such as mortgages or equity loans. You may also be asked for these documents:

- A current tax bill
- A real estate appraisal
- Copies of your mortgage

All states have local Medicaid eligibility offices where you can file applications. Many states also provide applications at different locations in your community, including Aging and Disability Resource Centers (ADRCs). You can also call your local Medicaid office to apply by phone. In most states, you can also apply online, or find an application online that you can complete and mail to your local office.

When to Apply for Medicaid

If you need long-term care, you should apply as soon as possible since it could take some time for your state to process your application. Generally, the date you become eligible is based on the date you apply for Medicaid (assuming you meet all of the eligibility requirements when you apply).

The Medicaid agency usually has 45 days to process your application. If a disability determination is required with your application, the agency can take 90 days.

Medicaid will review your eligibility status every year. During your yearly review, you may need to document your income and assets again, especially if either your income or assets have changed over the last year. Fortunately, the annual review process is usually much easier than the original application process.

Medicaid is not the easiest federal program to navigate. A Certified Medical Planner (CMP) can help you navigate current Medicaid rules and guidelines.

CHAPTER RESOURCES

- Find a certified medical planner in your area at www.payingforlongtermcare.com/plan

CHAPTER 9

Identifying Family Assets and Financial Resources

Most seniors entering long-term care may initially pay for their care using their own funds, and it's not uncommon for their adult children to pool funds to help cover care costs. Defining your family's assets is an important step in planning for long-term care costs. Here are some of the most common examples of family assets:

Cash and Cash Equivalents

- Checking and Savings Accounts
- Certificates of Deposit / Money Market Accounts
- Treasury Bills
- Social Security Income

Real Estate

- Primary Residence / Vacation Homes
- Rental Properties
- Commercial Properties
- Land

Investments

- Annuities
- Savings Bonds
- Mutual Funds
- Pensions
- Individual Retirement Accounts (IRAs)
- Retirement Plans/401K
- Stocks
- Life Insurance
- Company Ownership

Personal Property

- Artwork and Collectibles
- Motor Vehicles and Boats
- Electronics
- Jewelry/Gold/Silver
- Household Furnishings
- Equipment and Machinery

CHAPTER RESOURCES

- Download a user-friendly guide to calculating your family's assets at www.payingforlongtermcare.com/assets

PART II

CHAPTER 10

How to Pay for Care

We've discussed many of the different emotional factors and considerations involved with senior care—you now know that long-term care is extremely expensive and that there are lots of options out there and choices to make.

The following section of this book is dedicated to exploring different financial resources that can help you pay for care. Several of these resources may be possibilities that you never considered or knew were available to you. Every funding option has its pros and cons, and most families rely on a combination of payment sources to cover the costs of care.

It's important to remember that none of these financial resources are intended to provide care for decades. According to the U.S. Department of Health and Human Services, the average length of long-term care is roughly three years, and only one in five residents will need care for longer than five years. I share this with you to let you know that you are not likely planning for an extensive period of care, but instead determining how to get the best care for what may be three years.

SELLING THE FAMILY HOME

One of the biggest assets your loved one has is likely their house. Selling the house is typically the first thing families consider when trying to determine how to pay for long-term care. This can be a painstaking process, from downsizing to renovations to prepping the home for sale to dealing with realtors and showings. Not to mention the uncertainty of how long the house will take to sell. It's likely that your loved one has lived in their home for many years—sometimes a lifetime. The house, and all of the stuff in it, can be one of the most emotional parts of the transition journey.

Waiting for the Home to Sell Introduces More Risk to Your Loved One

By the time that a family is considering long-term care, their loved one has usually already shown declining health and the need for increased care. Waiting for the house to sell before taking that next step can cause delays in getting them care. The sooner that you can get them transitioned, the safer they will be. The sense of urgency to sell the home, coupled with not knowing where to start, can leave anyone feeling overwhelmed and at a loss about what the best option is.

Likely the house is full of stuff—a lifetime of memories—and it's an overwhelming and emotional process to pick out what's important, what's not, and what to do with all the stuff. You may not realize it, but to look through everything, decide which category it goes in (Keep It, Sell It, Trash It, Donate It, Pass It On) can take weeks, if not months. The average American home contains well over 300,000 individual items (clothes, kitchen items, basement items, garage items, books, pictures, furniture, and so much more).

So, you have decided that you need to sell the house and there is a lot to do: clean it out, arrange for some minor or major renovations, take photos, get it listed on the MLS, schedule showings, get it under contract, and close on the sale. Depending on your market and condition of the house, this can take anywhere from three to eight months.

You're probably saying to yourself right now, "This will be easy. We can clean it out in a couple of weekends." Maybe you know someone that can help repair that rotted wood, replace the carpet, or slap on some paint. If you have the time and experience rehabbing a house, this could be a feasible option. Maybe you're just a go-getter and don't have the experience but believe you can get this done. Or, maybe you're kidding yourself and this will turn into another one of those projects that drags on forever.

Have you ever told yourself that you're going to get a project done on your own house, you get all the materials you need for this weekend warrior project, and tell yourself, "This is only going to take a day or two, a month of weekends at the most?" The next thing you know, it's been half-complete for six weeks or more. Things usually take longer and cost more than we expect, especially when it comes to projects, rehabbing, or doing repairs.

As you decide how you're going to proceed, it is helpful to ask yourself if this is truly something that you have the ability and capacity for during this time, knowing that it is almost certainly going to take longer, and likely be a lot more expensive, than you think. As the saying goes, "You can only have two of the three: quality, speed, and price. You can't have all three." Assess your life, your schedule, and whether you have enough experience, time, and money to get the house ready for sale.

On average, most families spend months sorting and deciding what to do with the "stuff" before they even begin any work on the actual house. Once you've gone through the stuff you want to keep, what are you supposed to do with the rest of it? It's overwhelming and complicated. No wonder that a family's biggest asset can also be its biggest headache.

If your loved one is transitioning to long-term care, they are likely downsizing from a 2,000-square-foot space to a room that's roughly 150 square feet. In other words, space that will only fit a bed, a dresser, and a few other things. 90% of the stuff in the house simply has to go, which is rarely a fun process for you or your loved one. It's stressful and time-consuming, and I would argue that your time is better spent with your loved one who wants and needs your attention.

What to Expect

Now that you've decided to sell the house, you have a few different options. Each option has its own benefits and challenges, depending on your situation.

Option One: Have a family member buy the house.

This may seem easy and uncomplicated, but rarely is that the case. It still may be the best option in your situation if all members of the family have been preparing for the idea and are supportive of it. But how do you decide if it's the best option?

PLUSES

- This lessens the urgency to prepare the house for selling.
- The home and all of the stuff stays in the family.
- No commissions or real estate fees are involved.

MINUSES

- Deciding on a fair price with the entire family can be time-consuming and frustrating.
- Arranging for financing for the purchase can get complicated.
- It's a slower process to get equity from the house.
- You still need to clean out the house.

While it does provide a little more wiggle room for the family in getting things fixed up and cleared out, it only means that the burden is transferred to another family member. If all family members are in agreement about this, and it will not cause more problems than it solves, this may be the right option for you.

Option Two: List the house with a traditional real estate agent.

This is likely what you are leaning toward; it often seems like the only option. If the house is in good shape and market-ready condition, this may make the most sense and could be the clearest path forward. If you are wondering if this is the right path for your family, talk about the points below with your family to see how everyone feels about it.

PLUSES

- If the house is updated, in good repair, and has already been drastically downsized, this can be a suitable option.
- In a fast-moving market, with a ready-to-list, cleared-out house, you could close in 2-3 months.
- You can get top retail dollar with no money out of pocket for repairs (assuming the house is ready to list).

MINUSES

- You'll have to sink money into repairs and updates.
- You need to clear out and clean up the house.
- Interviewing, getting bids, and selecting a competent contractor will take time.
- You'll carry an ongoing cost for the home until it's sold: mortgage payments, taxes, insurance, and maintenance.
- Realtor commissions (typically 5% of the sale price) need to be paid.

If the family home is already ready to be listed, this can be a good option. If there are repairs or renovations that need to be done, updates that need to be made, or stuff that needs to be sorted and cleared out, this can be an extremely taxing job—and one that rarely pays off in time or money.

Option Three: Work with a certified senior transition "as-is" cash buyer.

You may not realize it, but there are professionals who are trained to work with families transitioning a senior into care and who will buy your house "as-is" with all of the stuff in it. No stress, no worries, and they can close in less than 30 days.

The most important part of this option is making sure that you find a trusted resource. I think we all have heard horror stories about real estate companies that prey on seniors or families in stressful situations. You have options here, and you want to work with companies that are credible, have experience in your market, are invested in training for buying houses "as-is," and understand the senior transition journey.

HERE ARE SOME QUESTIONS YOU CAN ASK:

How long have you been in real estate investing? Look for someone who has experience. This shouldn't be one of their first few home purchases.

How many houses do you buy per year? You are looking for someone who knows how to buy a house, has experience, has proof of funds, and will follow through on purchasing your house. The goal in that is that they will close on time, at the offered price, with no hiccups.

Do you typically wholesale houses or do you rehab? Partner with someone who has experience doing both. If a company says they are just wholesalers, there is nothing wrong with that, but the number they do a year could be an indicator of trust and credibility. The idea is to make sure the people that say they are going to buy your house really do and for their original offer. The last thing that you want is to have your loved one ready to move to long-term care but unable to do so because the buyer called last minute and said that they couldn't close. Or that they could close, but it would be for less than their original offer.

Do you have any certifications? Use a Certified Senior Transition "As-Is" Cash Buyer that has invested time and money to learn how to ethically and emotionally work with families to transition a senior into senior living.

PLUSES

- You can sell the house much faster and get funding for the care that your loved one needs.
- You can get your loved one care sooner.

- You don't have to worry about cleaning up the house and clearing out all of the stuff.
- You don't have to spend time being a project or contractor manager.
- You don't have to spend money to lose money (cost vs. actual returned value).
- You don't have to interview real estate agents, contractors, etc.
- You don't have to stage the home or prepare for showings.
- They have the training to work with families in a sensitive, respectful, and compassionate manner.
- There are no commissions or closing costs.
- The stress/burden level is low.

MINUSES

- You must choose a reputable company so that you don't get taken advantage of during an already stressful time and situation.

If you want to sell the house but don't want to sink time, energy, or money into getting it ready for market, clearing it out, and cleaning it up, this is an excellent option. You can get the money that you need to get your loved one care in a far shorter period of time compared to traditional MLS listing sales.

So, What Should You Do?

All three options could be ideal depending on whether they make sense for your situation and your family. You'll need to evaluate the options, your timeline, the carry cost for the house, and how quickly your loved one needs to get into care.

CHAPTER RESOURCES

- Download a checklist for getting your house ready to sell at www.payingforlongtermcare.com/guide
- Find expanded resources to help you sell your house at www.payingforlongtermcare.com/sell

VETERANS BENEFITS

The Department of Veterans Affairs (VA) pensions provide a monthly benefit for wartime veterans (or their surviving spouses) who need supplemental income. There are three types of pensions available for veterans and/or their spouses:

- *Basic Veterans* Pension and the *Basic Survivors Pension*
- *Housebound Pension*, also considered an "enhanced pension," which is specifically for people with limited ability to leave their homes
- *Aid and Attendance (A&A) Pension*, considered an "enhanced pension," which provides cash assistance to help in covering the cost of long-term care services or other medical expenses.

For long-term care planning, most veterans' families rely on the Aid and Attendance Pension. To qualify for the Aid and Attendance Pension, a veteran or his/her surviving spouse must meet the following eligibility requirements:

1. Military Service—The veteran must have served at least 90 days on active duty with at least one day during a period of war. The veteran must have received an honorable, general, or medical discharge. Unfortunately, service in the Army Reserve—unless called to active duty—does not qualify an individual for this benefit.

A certified copy or original discharge papers (DD-214) are required with an application for benefits. These documents will not be returned. A free certified copy can be ordered through www.archives.gov. There are private companies that can expedite the process.

Qualifying Periods of War

- **Mexican Border War**
  May 9, 1916–April 5, 1917
- **World War I**
  April 6, 1917–November 11, 1918
- **World War II**
  December 7, 1941–December 31, 1946
- **Korean Conflict**
  June 27, 1950–January 31, 1955
- **Vietnam War**
  February 28, 1961–May 7, 1975
- **Gulf War**
  August 2, 1990–present

2. *Medical Requirement*—The veteran must have a medical condition that requires assistance from another person. The applicant must meet at least one of these conditions:

- Needing assistance with performing daily living activities such as bathing, dressing, toileting, eating, or dressing

- Being bedridden—or spending most of the day in bed—because of an illness
- Residing in a nursing home, assisted living facility, or senior living facility due to physical or cognitive impairments that require an environment that will protect the applicant from the hazards of daily living
- Having extremely limited eyesight (visual acuity of 5/200 or less in both eyes or concentric contraction of the visual field to 5 degrees or less) The VA application requires certification from both a medical professional (MD, DO, PA, RN, etc.) and the care provider (home care aide or facility administrator) of the need for assistance with activities of daily living and/or to document medical conditions such as Alzheimer's disease, dementia, Parkinson's disease, macular degeneration, etc.

3. *Income Requirement*—The VA will consider total income from all sources less unreimbursed medical expenses. From there the monthly pension award is calculated. Income includes Social Security, pension, IRA distributions, interest, dividends, rental income, etc. This includes income paid to both the veteran and/or the spouse. Once that number is calculated, the VA will reduce income by the amount of unreimbursed medical expenses paid for services such as health insurance, home care aides, nursing homes, assisted living or similar communities, adult day care, etc. If the net income after deducting medical expenses is a negative number, the maximum benefit will be awarded. If there is some positive income left, the VA will award a partial benefit.

For example:

Income

Social Security:	$1,500
Pension:	$1,000
IRA Withdrawal:	$1,000
Total Income:	$3,500

Expenses

Medicare Supplement:	$250
Assisted Living Facility:	$4,000
Total Expenses:	$4,250

The net income for VA purposes is $0.00, so the VA will award the full benefit.

4. *Assets*—When determining eligibility, the VA considers all investments, savings, and other financial accounts (bank accounts, CDs, IRAs, mutual funds, stocks, bonds, etc.) as well as vacation homes, rental properties, and the land around your home if it exceeds two acres. Each year, the VA sets a maximum for assets. In 2021, the maximum assets an applicant can have is $130,772. Assets excluded include the primary home, personal vehicles and personal possessions.

Those with assets above the VA's limit can often become eligible with planning that complies with the VA's complex regulations. Make sure you seek the advice of a veterans financial planning expert. Simple mistakes can make an application ineligible for up to five years.

The VA pension is paid monthly and is tax-free. Calculating the pension benefit amount for a veteran or their surviving spouse can be complicated, since current monthly income and unreimbursed medical expenses (in other words, expenses not paid for by insurance) must be considered.

Surviving spouses of a veteran can apply for benefits based on the service of their most recent spouse. The regulations state that the marriage to the veteran must have lasted at least 365 days or resulted in the birth of a child and must have ended in the death of the veteran. Divorce from the veteran is a bar to entitlement. If the spouse remarried a non-veteran and the marriage started after 1971 and ended before 1990 and has not been remarried since, he/she can apply based on the service of the prior spouse.

While the application for benefits is complex, there are resources that can make the process easier. The key to a successful claim to the VA is a thorough application, proper supporting documents include discharge papers, marriage license, death certificate (if a surviving spouse is applying), financial statements, documentation of care expenses, and anything else that proves to the VA that the applicant meets the criteria above.

Once awarded, benefits will be deposited in the bank account of the applicant. This money is tax free, so there is no tax reporting.

CHAPTER RESOURCES

- For more information about how to apply and/or to find a VA-accredited representative, visit www.payingforlongtermcare.com/vet

LONG-TERM CARE INSURANCE CLAIMS

Long-term care insurance policies were designed to help cover the expenses of home care, adult day care, assisted living, memory care, skilled nursing, and hospice, as well as many other long-term care services typically not covered by health insurance or Medicare and Medicaid.

You would think that filing a claim would be fairly straightforward since all long-term care policies are essentially designed to work the same way. Unfortunately, this couldn't be further from the truth.

Families that attempt to file long-term policy claims on their own must understand the risks involved. The process of filing a claim is confusing and time-consuming. It's a process that many families must navigate while in "crisis mode" under emotionally charged and stressful circumstances. Without a thorough understanding of the policy's terms and the excessive amount of time required to manage the claims process, well-intended families often make mistakes that delay or jeopardize payments and care. As you now know, long-term care is expensive— when your loved one needs funding for immediate care, these payment delays can have a devastating impact on their quality of life.

If your parent or loved one is a long-term care insurance policyholder, they likely purchased their policy 15 to 25 years ago—and you probably didn't know much about it. It's a common scenario for the adult children (likely you or your brother or sister) to only learn about the existence of their loved one's long-term care insurance policy when it becomes critical to activate it.

> **Helpful Tip:** Before you start the claims process or contact your insurance company, it's critical to be aware of the most common mistakes made by families who attempt to file claims themselves.

Before You File a Claim: Understanding Benefit Triggers

It's important to note that owning a long-term care insurance policy does not guarantee benefits. Long-term care policies commonly use vague, confusing legalese that often trips up even the professionals. On that note, one of the most important first steps when filing a long-term care policy claim is understanding the policy's language with regards to its benefit triggers, a term used to describe when and how benefit payments begin.

Most long-term care policies start paying benefits once an assessment has determined that your parent or loved one needs help with two or more of the six Activities of Daily Living (ADLs) or if they are deemed to be cognitively impaired. Tax-qualified policies are required to include at least five of the six ADLs and must define a physical impairment as the inability to perform at least two of the ADLs without substantial assistance.

The six ADLs established by the Health Insurance Portability and Accountability Act of 1996 (HIPAA) are:

- *Bathing* (Getting into or out of the tub or shower)
- *Continence* (Control of bladder or bowel function)
- *Dressing* (Putting on and taking off clothing)
- *Eating* (Feeding oneself from a plate, cup, or table)
- *Toileting* (Getting to and from the toilet/practicing personal hygiene)
- *Transferring* (Moving into or out of a bed, chair, or wheelchair)

A licensed healthcare practitioner will need to certify that your loved one's inability to perform ADLs is expected to last at least 90 days.

Cognitive impairment is defined by the Centers for Disease Control and Prevention (CDC) as "when a person has trouble remembering, learning new things, concentrating, or making decisions that affect their everyday life." But the insured's cognitive impairment must be far more significant than simple memory loss. In order to qualify for benefits on a cognitive basis, the insured must be impaired severely enough that they require substantial supervision to protect them from threats to their health and safety. This needs to be documented in medical records by a licensed healthcare practitioner in such a way that satisfies the policy's language.

Once the benefit triggers have been met, the claimant—who must be authorized as a Durable Power of Attorney (DPOA) if they did not purchase the policy themselves—can initiate a claim. The insurance company will then approve a plan of care, and there will be an elimination period—typically 30, 60, 90, or 180 days after the benefit trigger occurs—before you start receiving payments.

Before You File a Claim: Understanding Your Policy's Elimination Period

In order to secure funding for your loved one's care as quickly as possible, it's crucial to understand the nuisances involved with the policy's elimination period. The elimination period (sometimes called the waiting period or deductible period) is similar to the deductible used in other forms of insurance. Measured in days, the elimination period refers to the time between when the benefit trigger occurs and when the policy will start paying benefits. During this time, the cost of services provided to your loved one or parent must be paid out of pocket.

Although your parent or loved one may have set the length of the elimination period when they purchased their policy, the insurance company determines how it functions. Insurance companies that require policyholders to receive paid care services during the elimination period will differ in how they count the days toward satisfying the period. Some policies only count the days on which services are provided, and others count all days while services are received.

> **Tip:** It's important to understand that the way that insurance companies calculate the elimination period can differ greatly. Most of the time, families leave money on the table by miscalculating the elimination period on current and previous care, especially when moving into long-term care. At the end of this chapter, there are some free resources that can help you to better understand this concept.

A simple example:
Barbara has a 60-day elimination period that counts only service days. On November 30, she starts requiring home health care services 3 days a week. It will take her 20 weeks (or roughly five months) to satisfy her policy's elimination period (3 days a week × 20 weeks = 60 days).

Note: Most of the larger insurance companies have a one-time only elimination period. In other words, once the period is satisfied, it never needs to be again.

Navigating the Claims Process

Considering the astronomical costs of long-term care, there are major benefits for insurance companies to have the claims process drag out as long as possible and scrutinize every reason to delay or deny benefits. In other words, every delay that the insurance company creates while you navigate the claims process helps them preserve their bottom line. And here is another ugly truth: If your loved one is considering long-term care, he/she is not likely in good health and nearing the end of his/her life. Who do you think benefits if the maximum policy amount is not paid out?

Unless you're a long-term care insurance expert or elder law attorney, long-term care policies are confusing for people like you and me to understand. Contract language and design, like many legal contracts, are written for the benefit of the company that created the contract, in this case the insurance company.

Most long-term care insurance policies are 20 years old…and so is the language. Because of this, the policy language is vague and outdated, and hard to understand if it still applies. Assisted living, for example, wasn't even a concept 20 years ago—today it's everywhere.

The next hurdle is the strict criteria for required documents, paperwork, and other elements to support the claim. You are mistaken if you think gathering medical records is easy; gathering these documents takes a lot of time and adds to the claims process mess. Language vagueness and document restrictions are simply more of the endless delay tactics that insurance companies use to avoid or delay paying out benefits. Missteps are very easy for any policyholder to make, and every misstep causes further delays.

Filing a long-term care claim also requires continuous follow-ups with various providers to ensure that the proper documentation is submitted every month. Confirming that the insurance company actually received the paperwork is problematic…and not just because the average call hold time is 45 minutes to an hour. Every contact made with an adjuster actually restarts the 30-day clock before the insurer is responsible for notifying the family of issues with their claim.

Support During the Claims Process

Families should never assume that the insurance company is on their side throughout the claims process. Adjusters are trained to make decisions with their company's best interests in mind—not yours. If you're struggling with the overwhelming burden of managing a long-term care claim, take a deep breath: there are resources available that will have your best interests in mind.

CHAPTER RESOURCES

- Learn the most common mistakes that families make during the claims process at www.payingforlongtermcare.com/claim
- Receive a free review of your long-term care insurance policy with expert feedback and advice at www.payingforlongtermcare.com/review

LIFE INSURANCE CONVERSIONS

Families often don't realize that converting a life insurance policy into a long-term care benefit plan may be an option. However, anyone with an active life insurance policy can transform it into a pre-funded financial account that disburses a monthly benefit to help pay for needs such as home care, assisted living, skilled nursing, and hospice. Unlike life insurance, this account is a Medicaid qualified asset.

How It Works

The conversion process transfers ownership of a life insurance policy from the original holder to an entity that acts as benefits administrator. Because the original owner no longer holds the policy, it won't count against your loved one or parent in the Medicaid spend-down process.

The benefits administrator assumes all responsibility for paying the monthly premiums on the policy to the insurance company, and agrees to pay the previous policyholder a series of monthly payments based on the value of their policy. These payments can then be used to pay for your loved one's or parent's long-term care.

THE PLUSES

- Most life insurance plans can be converted: whole, term or universal.
- There are no monthly premium payments, and monthly payout amounts are adjustable based on how many months you want to receive payments.
- Monthly payouts don't count against your loved one or parent qualifying for Medicaid coverage because a long-term

- care benefit plan is recognized by Medicaid as an acceptable spend-down during the five-year look-back period.
- A long-term care benefit plan is made up of "private pay" dollars, meaning it can be used to pay for any kind of care: home care, assisted living, skilled nursing, and hospice.
- A special fund is also set aside for future funeral expenses.

THE MINUSES

- Your loved one or parent must have an immediate need for an acceptable form of long-term care because monthly payments are made directly to a long-term care provider, not the previous holder of the life insurance policy.
- If your loved one or parent has a smaller policy ($10,000 or less), it may be to their advantage to keep their plan, or give it up in exchange for the cash surrender value. On the other hand, those with a life insurance policy with a large cash value built in (i.e., a $100,000 policy with a $90,000 cash value) may be better off taking that cash value.

What to Expect

There are no application fees or obligations to apply for a life insurance conversion, and the typical enrollment time is 30-45 days. Once a policy is converted by the owner, the Long-Term Care Benefit payments begin immediately and the enrollee is relieved of any responsibility to pay additional premiums.

FINANCIAL RESOURCES FOR PEOPLE WITH CANCER

You may have seen one of the commercials on television that claims that billions of dollars have been set aside to compensate victims of mesothelioma or asbestos-related lung cancer. That is actually true. There are $30 *billion* in cancer trust funds that have been earmarked to help pay for care for people who were exposed to asbestos. However, time is running out on the trusts as this money will go away in 3-10 years, depending on the particular trust fund. The good news is that filing a claim is a simple process and **most people will never even need to leave their home** to file a claim, much less go to court.

If you or a loved one has been faced with a cancer diagnosis, specifically mesothelioma or asbestos-related lung cancer, it's important to know that there may be money set aside to pay for care.

At the end of this chapter there is information on how you can assess your risk to see if you or your loved one would qualify to receive funds from these trusts.

How It Happened

After a surge of claims in the early 1990s, companies that had manufactured asbestos products from the 1950s through the 1980s were found to have poisoned entire generations of American workers and their families by using asbestos in their products. They had a known safer alternative to use in their manufacturing process—fiberglass—but chose to continue to use asbestos for the next 40 years because it was more profitable for the company by a few pennies per ton. Not only were those companies found to know about the dangers of asbestos, but it was also discovered that they went to great lengths to hide that risk from the very people that it would later come to affect—often decades later.

Hundreds of larger manufacturers of asbestos-containing products, as well as asbestos suppliers, declared bankruptcy. Due to the large numbers of claims against them, and the overwhelming number of claims that they knew would continue to grow for decades, they set up asbestos trust funds. These trusts were intended to cover the financial settlements and benefits owed to cancer victims based on occupational exposure to carcinogens. The establishment of the trusts legally prevented those companies from facing any more asbestos-related lawsuits. Anyone who has a claim of personal injury, caused by exposure to asbestos, was then able to file a claim against the trust to receive compensation.

Because of what is generally called "the latency period" of these cancers, **the disease often does not manifest itself until 20 to 70 years after the exposure.** Due to that delay in onset, mesothelioma and asbestos lung cancer are much more common in retirees. Families whose loved ones have been diagnosed with asbestos-related cancers are now confronted with the reality that the level, and cost, of care will likely be more than they can handle on their own. Filing a claim to access the trust that was established for that exact purpose is a commonsense way to pay for care that they need and deserve.

Did You Know?

- The average mesothelioma compensation is over $1 million. Trust funds rank different asbestos-related diseases based on eight "disease levels." Mesothelioma claims are ranked the highest and award the greatest amount of compensation.
- Claims are not only paid out to those who have been diagnosed with mesothelioma, but those with other cancers that are linked to asbestos exposure, such as liver, kidney, bladder, and colon cancers.

- Talcum powder is also known to be contaminated with asbestos, and individuals who were exposed may be eligible for compensation from the manufacturers and through the bankruptcy trusts.
- Asbestos trust funds review claims either through an expedited review or an individual review. Each process has its own criteria that must be met.

The Review Process

Expedited Review—Through an expedited review, the trust fund determines if a claim is valid through a set of pre-determined requirements that are available to the public. If a claim satisfies all of the requirements, it will not be disputed and will be paid at the fixed value and paid out quickly.

Individual Review—Fixed values from expedited reviews may not pay enough to cover all of an affected person's medical expenses. In these cases, an individual review may be requested.

In an individual review the evidence is evaluated and the claim is then assigned a monetary value. Those who request an individual review typically want to get more money from an asbestos trust fund due to the severity of their specific case.

Who Qualifies?

The occupations most at risk for developing mesothelioma disease after asbestos exposure include firefighters, construction workers, industrial workers, power plant workers, electricians, and shipyard workers. These workers regularly handled asbestos-containing materials in high volumes.

High-Risk Workspaces or Occupations That May Have Been Affected

Industrial Setting:
- Steel Mills
- Refineries
- Paper Mills
- Power Plants
- Shipyard or Navy Personnel
- Heavy Manufacturing Plants

Industrial Occupations:
- Pipe Fitter/Steam Fitter
- Machinist or Machinist Mate (Navy)
- Boilermaker
- Furnace/Kiln Operator
- Insulator
- Laborer
- Maintenance Mechanic

Outliers: If an affected person was employed by or an independent contractor in any of these entities:
- Any Insulating Company
- U.S. Steel
- Marathon Oil
- Shell Oil
- Caterpillar
- International Harvester
- General Electric / Westinghouse
- ComEd (Commonwealth Edison)
- Tidewater Construction
- Paul J. Krez Construction
- Iowa Illinois Taylor Insulation
- Union Carbide

The trusts are also to include family members of people who worked in environments where they were exposed to asbestos as claimants. Asbestos material often traveled home on workers' shoes and clothing, affecting their spouses and children. Many veterans were also subject to asbestos exposure in the military.

MEET PATSY—AN UNSUSPECTING VICTIM OF EXPOSURE
Patsy married at age 19, raised four children, and was a proud homemaker. Her husband worked for 25 years at a metal and plastic parts factory that used asbestos insulation in their products.

Recently, she had been diagnosed with peritoneal mesothelioma and wanted to see if she could get help covering her medical expenses and could get help transition her to an assisted care facility. She was frustrated because "I spent my whole life taking care of everyone else and I just don't know how to let people help me." Her diagnosis of mesothelioma could only be caused by asbestos and she could not imagine how she would have been exposed.

However, Patsy's exposure was easily explained. She was the victim of something called "take home exposure" to asbestos fibers. For 25 years she had done her husband's laundry and he had worked directly with asbestos on his job. The company did not provide uniform storage or a shower facility at the job site, so her husband wore his work clothes home. The asbestos fibers, which look like a gray dust but are too small to see individually, would attach to his clothes with tiny hooks and be released in the home environment. Patsy described how she would have to shake, sort, and pretreat his clothes, because "washers in that time were not nearly as good and they are now."

By doing her husband's laundry, Patsy was exposed to more than two decades of asbestos fibers and eventually developed mesothelioma. Despite all that she was going through and the seriousness of her diagnosis, her main concern was how her cancer would affect everyone else. She worried about her three daughters and her son. She worried that she would be a burden to them.

It was able to be proven that there was a large amount of asbestos at her husband's factory, and attorneys were able to scientifically show how the fibers were taken to her home and were then breathed in and swallowed by Patsy.

Thankfully, Patsy's settlements were large enough that she was not only not a burden on her loved ones, but she was also able to travel and continue to help and support her family—which was all she ever wanted to do.

What to Expect

Most people don't like the idea of lawsuits or lawyers in general. Many have never pursued any legal claim in the past. If they have, they often were overwhelmed with the process or amount that they ended up having to pay out of pocket. Your family will **not have to pay to file this claim**. Attorneys only get a fee, typically a percentage, if they actually win your claim and provide a benefit to you. If your claim is not won, you are not out any money. The best part? **You don't have to go to court, and often don't even need to leave your home.**

It may seem overwhelming to file a claim for these funds in addition to everything else that you have going on right now. Relax, take a breath, and know that there are professionals who will help you get the money you deserve to pay for the care that you or your loved one needs.

CHAPTER RESOURCES

- Answer a three-minute questionnaire to determine whether you or your loved may qualify for compensation from cancer trust funds at www.payingforlongtermcare.com/fund

REVERSE MORTGAGES

Reverse mortgages—which allow homeowners to borrow money against their home's equity—are becoming increasingly popular, especially for seniors who need help funding their plans to 'age in place.' In other words, your home equity can be tapped as another monetary resource. The cash flow generated from a reverse mortgage can help your parent or loved one remain in their own home longer. However, reverse mortgages aren't for everyone, and it's important to consult with a reputable FHA-approved lender who can assess your loved one's individual situation and needs.

Home Equity Conversion Mortgages (HECMs) are the only reverse mortgages backed and regulated by the U.S. Department of Housing and Urban Development (HUD). The Federal Housing Administration (FHA) insures the loan with a Mortgage Insurance Premium that the homeowner pays as part of closing costs—usually only giving up equity and not cash—and guarantees the homeowner and/or their heirs will never owe more than the home is worth when it is sold. No monthly payments are required, but they are always optional. The loan doesn't need to be repaid until the homeowner permanently leaves the home or passes away. If the home is sold for less than you owe, FHA will pay the difference with the Mortgage Insurance Premium you paid for up front. The home, and not the homeowner or the homeowner's heirs, is responsible for repayment.

How It Works

- If your loved one or parent is aged 62 or older and owns their home outright or has at least 50% equity, they may be eligible. The home must be their primary residence.

- Generally, seniors can borrow a maximum of roughly 70% of their home's value. The FHA updates the maximum borrowing limits annually, which are determined by county. The homeowner's age and equity owned are other factors that determine how much can be borrowed.
- Funds are paid by the lending bank in a single lump sum, made in monthly installments, or as a line of credit. The loan does not need to be repaid until the borrower passes away or moves out of the home for one full year. Typically, the home is sold before the lender is paid back the full loan amount plus interest.

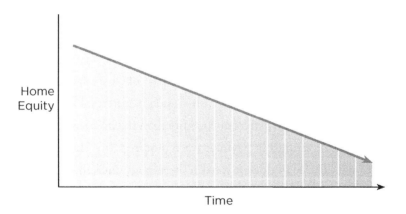

THE PLUSES

- There are no restrictions on how the money can be used.
- Reverse mortgages can be refinanced, payments can be made if desired and can be paid off with no prepayment penalty if plans change or the borrower wants to move.

- Homeowners will never owe more than their home is worth.
- There are no monthly payments on principal and interest.
- Credit checks are considerably less stringent than a regular mortgage. To qualify, the home must meet FHA property standards and flood requirements.

THE MINUSES

- Reverse mortgages can be complicated in Medicaid scenarios. If a client is working to qualify for Medicaid or other need-based programs like Supplemental Security Income, they must be careful to not take a lump sum and place it in an account that is a countable asset.
- Because of mortgage insurance, which protects the borrower, heirs, and the lender, fees are typically higher than a forward mortgage.
- The interest paid on a reverse mortgage cannot be deducted from your annual tax return until you pay off the loan.
- Since no monthly payments for principal and interest are required, seniors can risk foreclosure if they forget or neglect to pay property taxes, maintain property insurance, fail to pay HOA bills, etc.

When the homeowner passes away, the heirs typically have a set period of time to sell the home for fair market value, and two extensions are available. The sale of the home then repays the loan. If heirs are interested in keeping the home, they can pay the loan off. The bank does *not* own the home—it is the property of the homeowner or heirs and is subject to the lien payoff just like a traditional mortgage.

Reverse mortgages can be complicated and they're not right for everyone. It's a good idea to consult an FHA-approved HECM lender who understands their rules and regulations before making any decisions.

CHAPTER RESOURCES

- Find an FHA-approved HECM lender in your area who specializes in reverse mortgages for seniors at www.payingforlongtermcare.com/reverse-mortgages

HSA—HEALTH SAVINGS ACCOUNTS

Health savings accounts (HSAs) are often overlooked opportunities to help cover the costs of long-term care with tax-free money. If you or a loved one is currently paying into an HSA but aren't up to speed about all of its attributes, don't worry: You're in good company. A recent study by Voya Financial showed that only 2% of people were aware of exactly how HSAs work.

The good news is that there are a few ways that you can make the most of your HSA assets to help cover medical and long-term care expenses.

How It Works

A health savings account is a tax-advantaged medical savings account available to American taxpayers who are enrolled in high-deductible health insurance plans. An HSA offers a tax-friendly way to cover healthcare costs: The money in your HSA rolls over, or accumulates, from year to year and withdrawals are tax-free if used for qualified healthcare expenses.

You can deduct all contributions made to an HSA, earnings are tax-free, contributions made by your employer are excluded from your gross income, and distributions aren't taxed if you use them to pay for qualified medical bills. You can even hold on to your HSA account into retirement and use it tax-free to cover medical expenses.

By using the untaxed dollars in your HSA to pay for medical expenses, you are able to lower your overall healthcare costs while saving money for further care needs.

However, there are a few limitations and requirements to keep in mind, and they're adjusted for inflation every year. These limitations are related to the amount you can contribute to your HSA for the year, the deductible of your health insurance plan, and your yearly out-of-pocket expenses. If you're not in compliance with such restrictions, you'll lose your HSA tax savings for that year.

> Per the Internal Revenue Service (IRS), the maximum contribution amounts for 2020 are $3,550 for self-only and $7,100 for families. The annual "catch-up" contribution amount for HSA owners age 55 or older remains $1,000.

Using an HSA to Cover Long-Term Care Insurance Premiums

Few HSA owners know that it's possible to tap your HSA—tax free—to pay for qualified long-term care insurance premiums. However, the IRS will only allow you to pay for long-term care insurance with your HSA in certain situations. Insurance premiums are generally not treated as qualified medical expenses by the IRS, unless those premiums are for:

1. Qualified long-term care insurance (most LTC plans currently on the market are qualified)
2. Healthcare continuation coverage
3. Healthcare coverage while receiving unemployment compensation
4. Medicare and other coverage for those who are 65 and older

Because all deposits made to HSAs are tax-deductible, the amount you withdraw to pay for premiums is tax-deductible as well. However, it's important to note that:

- The long-term care policy must be a "qualified long-term care insurance contract" (most stand-alone LTC policies currently on the market are tax-qualified, but it's important to check with your insurer)
- The amount of HSA assets that can be withdrawn each year to cover long-term care insurance depends on your age. Those limits typically increase a bit each year.

Using an HSA to Cover Other Long-Term Care Costs

HSA funds can also be used to pay for:

- COBRA coverage
- Healthcare coverage while unemployed
- Medicare
- Other health coverage once you or your loved one is age 65 or older
- Qualified long-term care services

CHAPTER RESOURCES

- Download the questions you need to ask your health insurance company to see if you qualify for an HSA and find HSA providers in your area at www.payingforlongtermcare/hsa

FUNDING STRATEGIES TO PAY FOR IMMEDIATE NEEDS

Financial Planning for Those Who Are in Need of Care Now as Well as Those Who Are Pre-Planning for the Future

Most financial planners who specialize in long-term care planning will tell you that they typically help both the parents *and* their adult children. Once the 60-year-old son or daughter experiences what their parent is going through, they understand the importance of being prepared for their own futures. In this section we'll address both issues.

IMMEDIATE NEED OR CRISIS PLANNING STRATEGIES (NO PARTICULAR ORDER)

1) For those who are younger with significant medical issues, there is a product category called a **medically underwritten immediate annuity**. This is different from a traditional immediate annuity, which is a contract between the buyer and an insurance company to make payments for a specific period of time (e.g., 60 months or 120 months), for a lifetime (based on age), or for both (the rest of your life but at least 120 months). A medically underwritten immediate annuity considers not just your numeric age but also your health conditions, which can shorten your life expectancy significantly.

These medically underwritten products are commonly used when someone needs additional funding each month to pay for care. The family submits medical documentation to the annuity company. Based on that information, they assign a life expectancy, which can be significantly shorter than their age-based life expectancy, therefore increasing the monthly income by 5 to 50%. The ideal candidates for a contract like this are those who want peace of mind knowing that they can't outlive their money. The most common cases involved those with no trusted loved ones to manage the money and ensure that the bills are paid each month.

2) If you or your loved one has assets but would like to become VA benefit and Medicaid eligible as soon as possible, traditional immediate annuities are an excellent strategy.

Here's an example: Mary is 86 years old and going into assisted living with Parkinson's disease. She knows she could live a long time and is worried about exhausting all of her money on care and leaving nothing behind for her children. She has assets of $400,000. Her monthly income is $2,500 and her cost of care is $4,500 each month. Mary works with a planner with expertise in veterans benefits and Medicaid to set up the following:

Mary falls short $2,000 each month, so they establish a 60-month monthly income annuity, which costs $120,000, to make payments of $2,000 (plus some interest) each month for 60 months. This covers her monthly expenses. She keeps an additional $30,000 for emergencies and gifts her children the remaining $250,000 to hold in reserve for her. In three years, she is VA benefits eligible, and in five years she is Medicaid eligible.

Bridge Loans

Some financial service firms offer bridge loans to help cover the cost of long-term care for your loved one or parent while you wait for the sale of a home or for other benefits to kick in. By covering the financial gaps until your longer-term solution comes through, bridge loans can help prevent interruptions in your loved one's care.

How It Works

A bridge loan is a financing option that covers—or "bridges"—brief gaps in funding. These are loans—not grants—for families as they wait for funds to become available for care. Bridge loan funds can be available in as little as 24 hours and are designed to be paid off quickly, when your home sells or other benefits kick in. Generally, bridge loans are utilized for 6-8 months until funding for your long-term care plan is available.

Unlike traditional loans, a bridge loan is more like a credit card. You are approved for a larger amount depending on your unique situation and draw a specific amount each month to pay for care. This is beneficial because interest is paid only on the funds used, not the entire credit line.

Bridge loans can be helpful for seniors and their families in the following situations:

- *Moving into a different home.* A bridge loan can help cover the immediate expenses of moving into a new home while your current home is on the market.
- *Transitioning into an assisted living community.* There are several expenses involved with moving into a care community, including entry fees, monthly fees, and moving fees. Bridge loans can help cover these costs while you're waiting for the home to sell.
- *Waiting for veterans benefits to kick in.* Due to a lengthy application and approval process, veterans benefits can take as long as 18 months to become available. A bridge loan can provide a lump sum that covers the time from when the veteran's application was submitted to when it was approved.

What to Expect

- Eligibility for a bridge loan will involve considerations of the applicant's credit score, liquid assets, income, and home equity.
- A bridge loan is often made with multiple family members as co-applicants, and a poor credit score from any co-applicant can be offset by the others.
- Funds typically process quickly after approved and can be wired directly to the long-term care provider.
- Bridge loans aren't contingent on collateral, like a home or car, so the approval process is usually quick. It's often possible to have available funds within 24 hours of applying.

Keep in Mind

Bridge loans often have a bit of a higher interest rate than other financing alternatives, and there may be caps on the amount of the loan. This may not be a concern as the loan is typically less than a year and solves the problem of getting your loved one into care as soon as possible.

Be sure to weigh your financial options with a trusted financial planner or elder law attorney to make sure that a bridge loan is right for your situation.

Pre-Planning Strategies

Insurance and annuity products play a critical role in planning for long-term care expenses. If you are in your 60s and planning for way down the road or 80s and planning for five years down the road, there are options that can transfer some of the risk of your long-term care needs to an insurance company, providing peace of mind. Here are just a few ideas:

Life insurance products that were built to pay long-term care expenses more than paying a large death benefit. While there are numerous variations of these products, the most common example is the client makes a one-time payment to the insurance company, for example $100,000. The product will guarantee that if never needed for long-term care purposes, your heirs will get back at least $100,000. However, if you need long-term care such as assisted living, home care, etc., that product will pay out anywhere from $100,000 to hundreds of thousands depending on the product, age, time you've held the product, features you choose, etc. These products are excellent for anyone who can afford to set aside a lump sum of money for their care needs and is in good health.

Annuities with long term care provisions. Many annuity companies are now building into their products provisions to help pay for long-term care expenses. These features may be as simple as waiving any early withdrawal fees to doubling your income stream. Here is an example of how that might look.

Example: John is 70 and healthy. He deposits $100,000 into an annuity with a lifetime income rider. His intention is to leave the account untouched until he needs some care. At age 85 he requires care so he turns on the income stream. The company doubles his projected income, so he receives $46,000 per year for 2.5 years and then the company continues to pay out $23,000 per year as long as he lives. This could result in a significant return on investment with no stock market risk. These products can be a huge benefit to anyone with longevity in their family. Best of all, if he doesn't need care, his heirs will receive the entire value of the account when he passes.

There are several options when it comes to planning on paying for long-term care. The important part is to work with a financial planner who specializes in working with seniors or planning for senior care.

CHAPTER RESOURCES

- Find a bridge loan lender in your area at www.payingforlongtermcare.com/bridge
- Learn the questions that you should ask your financial planner at www.payingforlongtermcare.com/planners

PART III

CHAPTER 11

Researching Senior Living Options

If your family has made the decision that senior living is the best fit for your loved one, now it's time to dig in and find the best place for them. This is a large task in and of itself. At this point, that familiar fear of making a mistake may be creeping up again. But knowing *how* to research will help you keep the fear at bay and, most importantly, help your family to make an informed and confident decision for your loved one or parent. Here's what to do.

Assess First

For most families, the initial instinct is to head straight to Google and see what communities your loved one might like. Hold off on that. It's too easy to get overwhelmed that way, so don't start with a Google search. First, assess where things stand with your loved one or parent from a big picture perspective, not just the immediate need.

You want to choose a community that will be an ideal fit not only today, but tomorrow as well.

Answer these questions:

- What are the health issues and concerns?
- How is your loved one or parent's social and emotional well-being?
- Do they have any cognitive challenges or concerns?
- Do they have any mobility challenges?
- Can they still perform daily activities and tasks independently?
- Can they still maintain the house and/or yard?
- Do you worry about their nutrition and/or how they manage their medication?
- Can your loved one or parent still drive? Should they be driving?

Based on your answers you'll be able to narrow down the type of senior living that will fit those needs.

Take advantage of a free online assessment tool at www.payingforlongtermcare.com/assessment

Determine What's Most Important

Next, make a list of what's most important for your loved one or parent. If at all possible, your loved one should create this list.

Remember, most senior living communities provide meals, transportation, home maintenance, and activities as standard.

Beyond that, your list should include:

- *Non-Negotiables*—This could be something like the community must allow pets, offer private accommodations, or have plenty of outdoor space.
- *Location Preferences*—This may be as simple as wanting a community within a certain zip code, near a park, or in an area that's within walking distance to shopping, dining, and entertainment. That being said, it's more important to choose the living community that best matches your loved one's needs.
- *Lifestyle Preferences*—Understanding the social strengths of a community is critical. When a family has chosen the wrong community, one of the top two stated reasons for dissatisfaction is *"I don't fit in here."* If your loved one or parent is particularly social, you'd want to make sure the community has a full activity calendar each month.
- *Amenities and Services*—This could include multiple dining venues, onsite spiritual programs, or anything else that sets one community apart from the others.
- *Budget*—Enough said. This will clearly play a major role in the community you choose.

Start Your Research

With a clearer idea of what you want and need in a senior living community, it's time to start researching options. But, make sure to check online *and offline* resources to get the full picture. Here's what each can offer.

Online Research

Ideally, you'd look within the location(s) you prefer and then by type of senior living, or, vice versa if the location is flexible. Once you've identified communities, check out their websites to see how well each fits the rest of your needs and wants.

Always visit a community's website by typing in its website address to visit it directly. Be particularly cautious when searching for communities on Google. Many of the search results will actually be third party sites that could make your search far more complicated. These sites will ask you to fill out online forms to gather further information about your needs, then collect and sell your data to their contracted companies. Once your information is sold, you'll likely end up getting more phone calls than you ever bargained for from multiple different senior living providers.

> Before you fill out any online forms related to care communities, look at the website's address. Be cautious if its address looks anything like www.somecompanyname.com/thecommunityname. This is a third party site that is collecting your data. The best website addresses should look something like this: www.communityname.com/locations

At a minimum the site should offer links to videos, image galleries, and activity calendars. Many will also offer self-guided assessments and/or financial calculators as well as a range of blogs, articles, and guides on topics related to aging. Even if you end up not choosing a particular community, their resources could be extremely helpful going forward for your loved one or parent and for you too! And if available, sign up for a newsletter to get regular community updates.

Reviews and Reputation

Be sure to look beyond the community website and check for online reviews to get a gauge on the reputation of the communities in which you are interested. If you see consistent messaging about customer service failures, lack of leadership, or high staff turnover, move on. Note the dates of the reviews. If older reviews are negative and newer reviews are positive, you may want to reconsider. Visit their Facebook page and look over their comments and images. Is the community lively? Positive? Caring? In other words, is the community a place where you could envision your loved one living?

Offline Research

It's simple, nothing beats firsthand experience. The community will naturally put on its best face so make sure those who truly know what it's like will back up that perception. Always check with trusted advisors such as your loved one or parent's physician, attorney, financial planner, and/or spiritual leader for their thoughts and recommendations. They'll likely have great insight since they're "in the industry," so to speak.

Even better, speak with residents and/or their families for the communities you're interested in, if possible. There's no better way to get the inside scoop.

Tour the Communities

Once you've settled on two to three top communities, you'll want to tour them. When doing so it's best to compare the communities across the same criteria. This makes it so much easier to keep focused and helps you remember what you've seen later so it doesn't all run together. The timing of your visit matters: During mealtimes, you'll be able to observe the residents (and the quality of the food). Stop residents and staff and ask them about the community. Are they friendly? Are staff engaging with residents and each other? Access an activities calendar (which is usually posted on their website) to select a time when they're having an activity or class you'd like to observe.

Here's some general criteria to help and questions to ask as you compare communities:

Download a printable version of the community comparison sheet at www.payingforlongtermcare.com/comparison

STAFFING

- What's their reputation/rating?
- What is the resident to staff ratio (during the day and at night)?
- What level(s) and types of care are provided?
- What training and qualifications do staff members have?
- Is the staff friendly? Does the community feel welcoming?
- How has communication with the community been so far?
- Does there seem to be a high staff turnover rate?
- What are their hiring practices?

LIFESTYLE

- What types of activities are offered?
- What amenities are available?
- What is the dining program like? Is there a dedicated chef?
- Is transportation offered? When and where?

- Are pets allowed?
- Is there a daily schedule?
- How does the community encourage socialization?
- How often are housekeeping and laundry services provided?
- Do they accommodate diets (i.e., low-fat, low-sodium, gluten-free, dairy-free)?

CAMPUS

- What safety protocols and security features are provided? Does the community have a disaster preparedness plan in place?
- How are medical emergencies handled?
- What types of accommodations are available? What's the difference in cost?
- How is occupancy—high or low?
- Can residents personalize their space?
- How clean is the community?
- How's the location?

COST

- What is the monthly cost?
- What's included in the price? What services are add-ons?
- What are the payment options?
- Is there a security deposit or community fee? How much? Is it refundable or non-refundable?

How Senior Living Differs from Skilled Nursing

Although skilled nursing is provided in a community setting, it's much different than senior living. More commonly known as nursing homes, these senior care communities are specifically for people who need intensive, around-the-clock care. Nurses and aides are readily available, and doctors will make visits to the residents. In addition, occupational, physical, and speech therapists are often on staff. Additional ways nursing homes differ from senior living include:

- Accommodations—Nursing homes are primarily a medical setting so they feel more like a hospital. Residents typically live in small rooms, often with a roommate. On the other hand, senior living communities feature a range of accommodations from private apartments to free-standing cottages in some cases. The accommodation options also make it easier for couples to stay together in senior living.

- Lifestyle—Nursing homes do offer some activity programming. However, one of the main benefits of senior living is the focus on lifestyle and wellness. Communities offer a range of activities, outings, clubs, and classes as well as amenities such as a pool, a fitness center, and restaurant-style dining. Because of the level of care needed in nursing homes, the focus is more on physical health.

Follow Your Favorite Senior Living Communities

On social media of course! Most senior living communities are active on Facebook and Twitter as well as Instagram and YouTube. This is a great way to get a feel for the personality of the community and get insight into daily life for the residents.

Red Flags to Run From

Don't be shy about asking questions of the community at any point in the process. They should be happy to help and want you to be confident in moving your loved one or parent there. BUT, if staff isn't helpful, seems unfriendly or unhappy, acts impatient, double-speaks, or won't answer specific questions, consider that a big red flag!

If the Tour Isn't Enough

You may still be undecided about which community is best after the tour. In that case, consider attending some of their events. Most communities have regular events that are open to the public. Check out their calendar and attend an event for a better sense of the community. Many communities will allow a "trial stay" for an individual to live in a furnished unit and try it out for a period of time to see if the community is a good fit for them. The stay should be five to 10 days and ideally include a weekend to see the level of activity on the weekend.

What if I Choose the Wrong Community?

Sometimes the choice to move into a community needs to be made quickly and it doesn't end up being a good fit. These are difficult decisions to make. Keep in mind that your choice of community is never permanent: If it doesn't work or make sense anymore, it's certainly possible to transition to another one. Remember, it generally takes a minimum of 90 days for a new resident to settle into a senior living community.

CHAPTER RESOURCES

- Prepare for your loved one's care by evaluating their needs with a customized assessment tool at www.payingforlongtermcare.com/assessment
- Download a printable senior care community comparison sheet at www.payingforlongtermcare.com/comparison

CHAPTER 12

Making the Best Decision

Congratulations on making it this far in the book and taking the next steps toward the best care for your loved one. You now have information about care options and a better understanding of financial resources. But you may still be wondering how to make the BEST decision. According to *Psychology Today*, emotions are said to drive 80% of the choices Americans make, while practicality and objectivity only represent about 20% of decisions. As you move forward, do your best not to make any decisions based on emotions alone.

Let Go of Guilt
It's so hard. Maybe you've promised your loved one you'd never move them out of their home, yet their needs turned out to be greater than expected. You can't fault yourself for that.

You may feel as though you've failed at caregiving, but keep in mind that most family caregivers are ill-prepared for this role. You're undoubtedly juggling your own commitments as well, which makes this situation even more challenging. Providing your loved one with the quality of life they deserve should never be viewed as a failure. You're still looking after them, just in a different way.

Are you questioning the fairness of having your loved one or parent leave home at a time when they are struggling the most? Do you feel like it's asking too much of your loved one? Again, not if moving will give them the care they need and a better quality of life. You may both be surprised at the difference the right support can make. Trust yourself.

Lastly, you may wonder how you can enjoy a normal life when your loved one is struggling. This is one of the challenges that all of us face. It is important to remember that while these emotional struggles have existed forever, the resources that exist today are better than ever before. Navigating this journey alone is not the best plan of action. You are likely new to this. However, there are experts available who deal with these challenges on a daily basis. Senior care specialists understand what you're experiencing and can provide insights into the various paths ahead. With the options that continue to expand on a regular basis, your journey doesn't have to be one filled with guilt, but rather one filled with support, options, and new beginnings.

Think Objectively

When emotion and guilt are in the driver's seat, you're more likely to second guess your instincts. These tips can help you think more objectively.

Give Yourself Grace—Whether you feel guilt, disappointment, fear, frustration, relief, or all of the above, it's healthy to express those emotions and work through them. Consider talking to friends who've been in similar situations or look at support groups. What's most important is not to let those feelings consume you.

Think Long-Term—That is what we're talking about here, right? Long-term care. Rather than focus on the difficulty of the transition period (which may be much easier than you imagine), think about the long-term benefit for your loved one or parent.

Avoid Decision Fatigue—This occurs when you've expended your mental energy by considering your options over and over again. When this happens, you lose the ability to objectively weigh those options. Even though time may be of the essence when choosing senior care for your loved one or parent, it's important to allow breaks in the decision-making process.

Make an Educated Choice—How do you make the best decision? Do what you're doing now: learn, assess, and research. Being educated and getting your questions answered will help you to have more confidence and peace of mind in whatever choice you make for your loved one or parent.

Give It Time—It will likely take time for everyone in the family to adjust to the decision whether it's care at home or in a care community. During this process, focus on the positives such as the fact that you now have the chance to enjoy being your loved one's daughter, son, wife, or husband again!

> **The HALT Method**
>
> HALT is an acronym that stands for Hungry, Angry, Lonely, Tired. If you make decisions when you're experiencing any of these things, emotion wins 100% of the time. Stay nourished, take a deep breath, surround yourself with people whom you trust and love, and make sure you're well-rested.

Getting Everyone Onboard

You've finally made a big step toward the best approach for your loved one's care. What if the rest of the family or your loved one who needs care doesn't agree? That's a common scenario, but don't panic. If decisions are addressed strategically, they may even bring your family closer together. Here are some tips for communicating effectively and overcoming common challenges with your family.

Think about Your Family Dynamics

Before trying to come to a consensus, consider your approach. What is your family's typical communication style? Does your family confront issues head on and then hash them all out? Or does your family have a tendency to avoid confrontation while silently seething? Consider how your own communication style differs from the rest of the family. Understanding your family's communication dynamics—and your contribution to these dynamics—can help resolve potential issues more quickly and effectively.

Stay in the Present

Even if everyone gets along now, it's common for siblings to have unresolved tensions from childhood rivalries. There's nothing quite like the stress of deciding on a parent's care to reignite old feelings of resentment. It's extremely emotional to witness a parent or loved one's health deteriorate, and it often magnifies emotions such as:

- Anger or resentment
- Hostility
- Fear
- Sadness and grief
- Denial
- Guilt

Above all else, though, this needs to be a time for putting past arguments behind you and focusing on your loved one's care.

Come Together by Focusing on the Goal

It's important to keep everyone focused on a specific goal for maintaining your parent or loved one's quality of life. One of these goals should be keeping them as safe, healthy, and independent as possible while maintaining their dignity. By shifting all focus toward a common goal and staying open-minded, families will work far better as a team, even in the face of stress or misunderstandings.

Realize This Is More Than One Conversation

Decisions about long-term care for a loved one or parent are some of the most important that you can make as a family. So, if you're planning on just having one conversation to square everything away, there are likely to be issues left unresolved. What you're really striving to do is to create an open, honest dialogue about what your loved one or parent needs and wants moving forward, as well as how their care can support those needs.

To that end, your first family meeting should be about opening the lines of communication (and setting some of those "play nice" goals). That's why you should invite all siblings, spouses, and other relatives who will be affected—and of course your loved one or parent too!

Distance shouldn't prevent anyone from participating, especially with options such as video conferencing or tech apps that facilitate collaboration. Use these tech apps and a calendar to stay organized and on task.

Communication Dos

- *Create Talking Points*—This not only keeps the discussion focused, it can also help you remember everything you want to say should the conversations get heated or emotional.

- *Show Empathy and Patience*—Remember that the person this is most difficult for is your loved one or parent. Chapter Two discussed common aging fears they may have, so it's crucial to take their perspective to heart.
- *Involve Them*—Again, the more your loved one or parent is involved in these decisions, the more confident they will feel about them. It can help to frame the discussion around questions about their needs and wants if possible:
  - What can we do to help you stay independent?
  - Do you still enjoy cooking?
  - How do you feel about driving?
  - Would you like more opportunities to socialize?
  - How do you feel about taking care of the house and yard?
- *Encourage Questions*—The best way to have an open dialogue is if no questions are off the table. Have your loved one or parent, as well as other family members, share their questions and concerns about senior care.

Communication Don'ts

- *Dictate a Plan to Anyone*—Even if you think you're in the best position to make the decision, everyone should be included in the process to have any hope of agreement, especially from your loved one or parent—they will be affected the most by these decisions.
- *Parent Your Parent*—Yes, the roles may have been somewhat reversed. However, they are still your parent and deserve to have a voice. Share your concerns, but make sure they're respectful. Otherwise, they likely won't be open about their true feelings and they'll be much more resistant to your opinion.

- *Scare Them About the Future*—Stoking fear never helps. Share concerns in a way that's collaborative about your loved one or parent's care and future. No one in the family will feel comfortable about decisions made from fear.

If You Just Can't Agree

If you and your family are still at an impasse after everything is said and done, it might be time to enlist the help of a neutral third party like your loved one or parent's physician, a case manager, social worker, therapist, or even their spiritual leader to see if they can offer a fresh perspective.

Give Everyone a Voice

This can't be overstated. Often there's a child, significant other, or sibling who is closest to the situation. Maybe they've been in the caregiver role or maybe they simply see your loved one or parent the most. This gives that person the inside track—because of this, it will likely make sense that they take the lead in discussions. But that doesn't mean that the rest of the family's input isn't just as important. Everyone should feel valued and heard to foster a spirit of collaboration in these important decisions.

CHAPTER 13

Strategies for Successful Transitions: In-Home Care and Senior Living

Transitioning into an assisted living community is often a highly emotional shift for seniors and their families. Their generation typically lived in the same home for decades, and their home may hold a lifetime of memories spent with their spouse and children. It's never easy to let go of your past, personal possessions, and independence. There are several things that you can do to make this lifestyle transition run as smoothly as possible, and ease some of the stress on your loved one and family.

Include the Community

It's important to care communities that your loved one or parent feels at home with them. Here's how they can help:

- Ask them for recommended resources that can help; i.e., moving companies and professional downsizing specialists.
- Arrange an in-home visit from the community. A staff

- member will visit, get to know your loved one or parent, learn their needs and preferences, and answer any lingering questions you may have.
- If possible, visit the community often with your loved one or parent to have a meal, participate in activities, and get to know the staff as well as their new neighbors.
- Ask your loved one to visit residents with the same apartment style and size to see the furniture layout and gather ideas about how they'd like to arrange their own space.

Learn What to Expect

It's always helpful to know what's ahead. Typically, once you put down a deposit, an assessment will be scheduled (unless you are moving into independent living) to ensure the senior living community can provide your loved one or parent with all the care they need. This assessment also determines any additional costs outside of the standard rent. For example, there are communities that include some care within the monthly fee and others separate rent and care. Every state regulates senior living differently, and the state determines what care can and cannot be provided.

Following the assessment, you will schedule a lease signing with the executive director and will typically need to bring paperwork that includes:

- A physician's clearance form
- Insurance, Medicare, and Social Security cards
- Legal documents such as Healthcare Proxy, POA, and DNR paperwork

Plan Their Space

This can give your loved one something to look forward to and get them more involved and invested in the process. Simply ask the community for a copy of the floor plan. Many communities also offer videos, interactive floor plans, and room planners online that can help you visualize how to set up the space.

Decide What to Bring

Your community may provide a list, but just in case they don't, plan for these items:

- *Comfort Items*—Bring your loved one or parent's favorite blanket and pillows along with sheets, bedspread, and a clock.
- *Personal Care*—Make sure they have a toothbrush, toothpaste, hairbrush, and comb, as well as a shaving kit for men or cosmetics for women. Include any other personal grooming items in addition to bath towels, hand towels, and wash cloths.
- *Clothing*—Bring clothes that are comfortable to wear and easy to get on and off. Also bring them rubber-soled shoes to help prevent falls. Also pack undergarments, pajamas, socks, robe, and slippers.
- *Favorites*—Pack photos, paintings, keepsakes, personal items, and perhaps even some favorite furniture pieces if allowed, plus favorite snacks, books, and/or music to make it feel even more like home.

Moving Day

The day will go much smoother if you:

- *Have Everything Ready*—All new resident paperwork should be complete, and your loved one or parent should ideally know their way around the community and be familiar with its policies.

- *Set Up Their Space*—This is one of the first things you should do; they'll feel much more at home once they're unpacked and settled in. Also, share some of their personal preferences with the staff if possible, such as their favorite scent or the name of their favorite sports team. This can help build rapport and they may even have some things in common.

- *Help Them Connect*—Senior living communities typically have new resident ambassadors (or some type of buddy system) to help new residents feel welcome. Ask the community if they don't mention this. Remind your loved one that the residents they meet have been in their shoes, and that asking them for tips can be a great conversation starter!

- *Get Them Involved*—Finding them some activities to look forward to will go a long way in easing the transition. So, make sure to get the community's activity calendar so your loved one or parent can see what's available.

- *Try to Stay Positive*—This will help your parent or loved one to do the same. Focus on the reasons you chose senior living and/or that particular community (i.e., the peace of mind in having help available 24 hours a day, amenities, outdoor space, spacious rooms, etc.)

After the Move

The first 30 days after the move to senior living are key. A transition like this isn't something most people can process overnight so you or your loved one or parent will likely experience some highs and lows. What's important is that you give them and yourself time and avoid rushing to judgment too quickly on whether or not things are working.

Be There

As simple as it sounds, this is one of the best things you can do to reassure your loved one, and perhaps yourself, that you're still just as much of a part of each other's lives. Visit and talk with them as much as you can. It can also help to preschedule times for visits or calls on the calendar so they can have even more to look forward to. Encourage other friends and family members to do the same.

Getting Social

Many seniors have the ability to utilize technology such as Facebook. Something as simple as creating a private Facebook group for your family can be an effective way for your loved one to feel connected:

- Create a Facebook group
- Add your family members and friends
- Encourage them to share stories, photos, and life update in the group

CHAPTER 14

How Technology Can Help with Companionship and Safety

While you likely don't have to be sold on the benefits of technology in everyday life, you may not realize how helpful it can be to your loved one or parent—specifically when it comes to companionship and safety. Even if they aren't particularly tech-savvy, advancements in technology mean it's increasingly easy to use as well. Here's how tech can help either at home or in a senior care community.

Connection

Pew Research Center reports that 53% of Americans over age 65 now have smartphones. If your loved one isn't one of them, it may be time to make the leap, as smartphones are ideal to help keep them connected to friends and family through video chat apps. Even Zoom works well on a smartphone. Helping them access (and learn to safely use) social media sites like Facebook can help them stay in touch with an even wider network of family and friends, reducing the sense of loneliness that many seniors feel as they age.

Fitness

In previous chapters we talked about the importance of fitness for your loved one or parent. One way to help them stay fit is using wearable technology. An AARP study found that 45% of respondents 50 years or older had increased motivation for healthier living after six weeks of wearable activity or sleep tracker use. In addition, 67% felt that such wearables were beneficial.

Great examples are Fitbit and the Apple Watch. With Fitbit you can track activity, sleep, food, weight, and more. The Apple Watch 4 takes it further with the ability to generate an ECG that you can share with caregivers and health providers to monitor their heart for irregularities.

Help with Daily Tasks

If your loved one or parent struggles to complete chores like vacuuming, or if it's hard for them to keep track of things like their keys or wallet, technology can help there too. Robotic vacuums and mops like Roomba can take care of the cleaning using programmable features and sensors to move around furniture. Many models can also be programmed from the app to clean on certain days and times so they don't even have to remember to turn it on.

There are also a range of voice-activated assistants like Amazon Echo and Google Home that can help your loved one or parent make grocery lists, set reminders, play music, answer questions, and even turn on lights, appliances, and the TV in some cases. Depending on the device and how "smart" their home is, the options are nearly unlimited. There are also senior specialty apps that help with tasks as well as safety. They can offer medication reminders, cognitive assessments, making calls to family, and even 911 if needed. See the resource section for a list of apps and devices.

Apps like Tile can help them keep track of important items like their keys, wallet, and phone. Simply download the app, attach a "tile" to the item to keep track of, and, if they lose it, Tile will play a tune to help your loved one or parent find it!

Safety

Falls. A seemingly benign word that typically brings up thoughts of skinned knees and bruised elbows. However, a fall means something entirely different for the growing population of senior citizens. In short, a fall can be a death sentence. If a senior falls and breaks a hip, the average time from the fall to death is *one year*. The National Council on Aging considers falls to be the "#1 health risk facing senior citizens today."

Medicare representatives say that falls cost them more than any other injury or illness when considering all the downstream effects. Most of us assume that falls happen to someone else's loved ones. However, a senior will typically fall four times before there is any documented injury or hospitalization. Once that injury occurs, the prognosis is grim and the likelihood of being able to live independently drops dramatically.

Despite the doom and gloom surrounding the aftermath of a fall, particularly one that involves an injury, there is hope. The human body is an incredibly resilient and adaptive organism throughout the aging process. Look no further than Svend Stensgaard, who, at the age of 93, can deadlift more weight than the average American male, or Edith Traina, a 90-year-old from Tampa, who competes in weightlifting competitions! Beyond weightlifting there is Fauja Singh, who at 101 years young finished the Hong Kong 10km race in 92 minutes. Or Maurine Kornfield, who, at the age of 97, regularly competes in swimming, often outpacing people decades younger than her.

While these "larger than life" examples may not be applicable to everyone, I think many would agree that the great-grandma who can still play with her great-grandchildren is just as much of a champion! Almost everyone has the chance to become more mobile, more autonomous, and more independent. Sometimes that can be difficult to believe. "Can I really do that?" is a question asked far too often. Breaking down this barrier can result in massive improvements to quality of life, and Paul Yerhot has seen it in action.

Paul Yerhot, DPT, at the Mayo Clinic enjoys bringing his sports medicine and athletic background to the senior citizen world. His experience has shown him that athletes and seniors often have higher motivation levels than one might guess, and that the progress of a senior, especially one who has a high fall risk, can be much easier to see. He recalls a particular patient who went from wanting to be confident walking to asking about playing tennis again 12 weeks later! With many primary care physicians not having comprehensive focus or strengths in fall prevention exercises, there is a disconnect for those who "see their doctor" but don't consult with a movement specialist like a physical therapist. This disconnect in the typical health care process is something that can be addressed through implementing technology solutions like a virtual fall-prevention program.

There are many different options for finding opportunities to lower one's fall risk as a senior. SARA (Strength Autonomy and Resilience Assistant) is focused on this area of health care with an individualized focus. Seniors complete an intake survey, then receive a set of assigned exercises for their individual needs. These can be done at home, and even with their loved ones. Over the course of the 12-week program, they track and report their progress. The exercises generally take 15-30 minutes per day and are performed at least three times per week at times that fit your loved one's schedule. However, the vast majority require an in-person or synchronous component, meaning that to participate a senior either has to go to a facility or attend a video call at a specific time. That can be a roadblock to many seniors and their families, who may not be able to facilitate this on a regular basis. While these types of programs can be somewhat beneficial to most seniors, they are not precise enough to address the specific issues of each individual.

With all the developments in technology, and a new set of innovations within the fall prevention space, seniors no longer have to settle. The development in technology provides a more individualistic approach for each senior while also monitoring their safety. Devices that monitor seniors in their homes can detect if a fall has occurred and can alert 911 as well as emergency contacts that are listed within the app. There are apps that are geared toward assessing each senior's fall risk through a short questionnaire. Then, with that data, it builds a unique fall-prevention program for each person that evolves as the senior "levels up." There are also apps that can keep track of medications with personalized reminders, drug interaction warnings, and refill reminders. This also promotes better communication (as well as accuracy) with healthcare providers because it allows your loved one or parent to easily provide complete medication lists.

There has never been a better time to be a senior in America. The dramatic increase in Medicare Advantage enrollment, which is expected to continue with an estimated growth of 40% over the next five years, coupled with the huge gains in technology, have created an incentive alignment among payers, providers, and patients to attack the issue of falls, and an increased ability to do that using technology. All of these market forces create a "perfect storm" for innovation that will ultimately improve the lives of seniors.

Transportation

One of the biggest challenges for seniors and their families is transportation. Whether your loved one still drives or not, technology can help them get to where they need to go safely. If they drive, make sure their car and/or their smartphone has GPS navigation and that they can use it. There are apps that can alert you when your loved one or parent is on the go, allows you to know their location, and feature automatic crash detection as well as automated SOS features. If the senior in your life does not drive, they still have options. There are paratransit programs that serve seniors, and, if they qualify, the service will pick them up at their home and take them to doctors' visits, the grocery store, and other essential places. Additionally, let's not overlook ride sharing options such as Uber and Lyft.

Teaching Tech to Seniors

You may be worried that your loved one won't be able to use the technology described. But this can be as simple as a tech-savvy family member or friend teaching them. Or, ask the grandkids—that could be a fun way for them to connect. What's more, your local senior center, local public library, local university, or local computer stores may offer resources as well. Senior care communities also regularly host events that can help them learn more about technology.

Technology Made for Seniors

Technology is more suited for senior use now than ever before as smartphones, as well as tablets and e-readers, feature large screens, voice capabilities, and the ability to navigate by touch.

Tech in Senior Living

Not only can technology help your loved one or parent at home, it can also be an advantage in the senior care community you choose. Many are incorporating technology into daily life in the community, from "smart" features in residences to increasing the options residents have to stay engaged and connected. There are a lot of third-party emergency response systems that can help with medication reminders, perform cognitive assessments, and even offer companionship through interactive apps. They can offer personalized care and better-quality monitoring. Some even qualify to be paid for through insurance.

CHAPTER RESOURCES

- Find innovative apps designed specifically for senior safety and companionship at www.payingforlongtermcare.com/connect

CHAPTER 15

Mental Health Resources for the Family and the Senior

As we've talked about throughout the book, whether you're the senior or a family member there's plenty of stress involved at any point in this process. This will be the case even after the transition to senior care. While we all know that stress is unhealthy, you may not realize the risks it can pose. Here's what you should know and where you can turn to for support.

The Impact of Stress on the Mind and Body

The body's stress response is not intended to be continuously engaged. That's why prolonged stress can begin to negatively affect both your physical and mental health. According to the American Psychological Association, 66% of people regularly experience physical symptoms of stress and 63% experience psychological symptoms.

Physical Impact Can Include:

- High blood pressure
- Increased risk for heart disease
- Weakened immune system

- Insomnia or sleeping too much
- Heartburn and/or indigestion
- Obesity

Mental/Emotional Impact Can Include:

- Anxiety and/or depression
- Feeling overwhelmed
- Irritability or anger
- Lack of motivation or focus
- Restlessness

What You Can Do About Stress

Rather than sweeping your feelings under a rug and trying to push forward, it's important to tackle stress head-on. These feelings typically won't resolve on their own, especially if the source of the stress remains. Try these tips:

- *Take time* to be with your friends and family and do the things that you enjoy.
- *Get back to the basics* like making sure you eat well, drink plenty of water, exercise regularly, and keep up with preventative health visits.
- *Relax and disengage* by meditating and/or spending time in nature. Quieting your mind can have a major impact on stress reduction.
- *Accept what you can't control* and focus on what you can. You'll find there's a real freedom in that.

- *Practice gratitude* by keeping a daily gratitude journal that you can reference when you're feeling particularly stressed.
- *Be kind* by actively looking for opportunities to help others. Practicing kindness and compassion has a positive impact on you and everyone around you.
- *Volunteer* to help others. Giving to others can help protect your mental and physical health and provide you with a sense of purpose and fulfillment.
- *Find renewed purpose* by pursuing old hobbies or getting involved with causes that are important to you. Investing in yourself can be empowering and liberating.
- Keep in mind that if your stress begins interfering with your ability to complete daily activities, you should call your healthcare provider.

It's Okay to Need More Support

Asking for help is one of the hardest things for many of us to do, because we fear being perceived as weak or vulnerable. The reality is that asking for help is an indication of emotional strength. There are a number of resources to which you can turn for advice and support. Find a safe space to share your experiences and build community with those who understand what you're going through. Ultimately, there is nothing more calming than spending quality time with another person who makes you feel safe and understood. This type of human interaction actually triggers hormones that counteract the body's "fight or flight" response.

Support for the Family

Even though you realize that their quality of life (and yours) will ultimately be better, choosing a senior care community is an emotional and stressful time. These resources can help:

- Family Caregiver Alliance—caregiver.org
- Alzheimer's Association—alz.org
- AARP Online Forum—community.aarp.org
- National Alliance on Mental Illness (NAMI)—nami.org

Support for Your Loved One or Parent

You can support your loved one by visiting them and keeping them in close contact with the community. Remember, you still have a vital and active role in their care and their life. Care communities can be great resources for support—and not just for your loved one who resides with them. They likely offer support groups, educational programs, and referral services for your entire family as well.

CHAPTER 16

Healthy Aging Through Nutrition and Exercise for Seniors

While there's no fountain of youth (unfortunately!), there are measures you can take to keep yourself as healthy, active, and independent as possible. This certainly isn't news, but once you're on the other side of choosing senior care for your loved one, the perspective on these preventative measures often changes. We realize how precious health and independence truly is and how much your well-being impacts your family. As healthy aging becomes a top priority, these nutrition and exercise tips can guide you.

Nutrition Tips

You've been advised to make healthy eating choices your whole life, but nutrition takes on a whole new level of importance as you age—along with a new complexity. You may have specific dietary needs related to health conditions, medications, bone health, gut health, and immune function as well as slower metabolism. Your palate may even change! Here's how to make it easier:

Diet Recommendations from the National Institute on Aging:

Daily servings for seniors
- Fruits—1½ to 2½ cups
- Vegetables—2 to 3½ cups
- Grains—5 to 10 ounces
- Protein foods—5 to 7 ounces
- Dairy foods—3 cups of fat-free or low-fat milk
- Oils—5 to 8 teaspoons
- Keep solid fats, added sugars, and sodium (salt) to a minimum

Remember to hydrate! Typically, adults need around 64 ounces of fluid each day (through beverages or food), but that amount can vary with heat, strenuous activity, medications, and health conditions so ask your doctor about what's best for you.

Understanding Nutrients:

Beyond knowing how much to eat, you should also know which nutrients affect specific aspects of your health.

- Vitamin D and calcium help to prevent osteoporosis and can be found in fish, fortified cereal, eggs, and juice.
- Vitamin B12 helps with energy levels and can be found in beef, liver, mackerel, sardines, red meat, yogurt, and fortified cereals.
- Fiber helps with maintaining digestive health, lowering cholesterol, and stabilizing blood glucose levels. It can be found in beans, vegetables, fruits, nuts, and whole grains.

- Omega-3 fatty acids like flaxseeds, chia seeds, salmon, walnuts, tofu, shellfish, canola oil, navy beans, Brussels sprouts, and avocados as well as flavonoid-rich foods like dark berries, cocoa, tea, soy, citrus fruits, and red wine can help with immune function.
- Probiotics promote gut health and can be found in yogurt, pickles, some cheeses, and sauerkraut.
- Seasonings such as garlic powder, onion powder, dill, paprika, pepper, citrus, and fresh herbs also offer a substitute for salt to help reduce your sodium intake.

To learn how to put all this together to create healthy meals, visit ChooseMyPlate.Gov. The site also has resources to help you better understand how to read nutrition labels.

Shop Smarter:
It's important to plan your weekly menu in advance to avoid impulse buying and to stay on budget. What's more, take advantage of sales to stock your pantry with canned vegetables, beans, fruits, and dried foods such as rice and pasta. Also, buy in bulk when you can and then freeze the items in smaller portions that you can thaw and cook later.

Or, skip shopping at the store altogether and enjoy the convenience of online ordering with curbside pickup and/or delivery at your local grocery. Meal delivery services are also becoming increasingly popular if you have the budget for it. See Resources below for a link to meal delivery services in your area.

Cooking for One or Two:
Don't be sucked in by highly processed frozen meals or constant takeout if you're cooking for one or two. Most of the time, these types

of meals are high in salt, fat, and sugar. It's easier than you may realize to keep your diet healthy.

- Make large meals to freeze into smaller portions with menu ideas that include soups, stews, chilies, roasts, casseroles, and any kind of slow-cooker meal. You can even make fresh side dishes each time you thaw out a portion to keep it interesting.
- Make your sides multipurpose. For example, have rice as a side for one meal and use it for a casserole the next. Have chicken as a main dish in one meal and use leftovers in sandwiches the next day.
- Have a dedicated cooking day a couple of times a month where you make several meals to portion and freeze. This helps you avoid having the same meal multiple times in a row.

Always remember to write the date on the packages you freeze and move older items forward so the food doesn't spoil. A Sharpie works best.

Exercise Tips

The National Institute on Aging recommends seniors do a minimum of 150 minutes of moderate-intensity physical activity each week in sessions of at least 10 minutes duration across four categories of exercise: endurance, strength training, balance, and flexibility. To break this down, you might exercise approximately 20 minutes per day, seven days per week; 30 minutes per day for five days per week; or 50 minutes per day for three days per week. The breakdown can fit whatever is most convenient for you. Here are recommendations for specific exercises in each category:

- *Endurance Exercises*—Try brisk walking, dancing, jogging, swimming, biking, or even group sports such as tennis or basketball. Even yard work or climbing stairs count, as long as it's an aerobic activity that increases your breathing and heart rate. You might consider getting a pedometer or Smartwatch to track your steps.

- *Strength Training*—Just like it sounds, these exercises are focused on improving your muscle strength. You should exercise all major muscle groups (shoulders, arms, chest, stomach, back, hips, and legs) two or more days a week. But be sure to not exercise the same muscle group two days in a row. Again, this doesn't need to be complex: You could simply keep some two-pound weights handy for arm curls while watching TV, do some pushups while your coffee is brewing in the kitchen, or do squats while you wait for the microwave to warm your food.

- *Balance Exercises*—The CDC reports that nearly a third of seniors fall each year, and these falls are the leading cause of home injury. However, you can work to improve your balance through exercises like standing on one foot or heel-to-toe walking. Also, check for local Tai Chi classes or find one online as it's also an effective way to reduce your fall risk.

- *Flexibility Exercises*—Keeping your body limber through stretching gives you more freedom of movement. Anyone who has experienced aches and pains when standing after sitting for long periods, had trouble bending down, or suffered from a stiff neck will appreciate this. You can find neck, shoulder, and upper arm stretches as well as calf stretches online. Yoga is another option.

Bonus Tip: One of the best things you can do is to make exercising fun. You're much more likely to keep it up that way! You could even look at it as a social opportunity. Join classes at your local senior center or gym or start a walking club with friends. It can also help to incorporate movement into things you already love to do, such as gardening or interacting with your grandchildren at the park. Listening to music, podcasts, or audio books while exercising can make the time pass more quickly.

Double-Bonus Tip: Always make sure you spend about five minutes before and after you exercise to warm up and cool down. This gives your muscles a chance to prepare for exertion and can prevent injury and soreness later.

Nutrition Apps

Even once you make your health a priority, it can be hard to keep everything on track. These apps can help:

- Food Network in the Kitchen—Offers thousands of recipes in categories such as Healthy, Weeknight Dinners, and Quick and Easy along with on-demand cooking classes and tutorials.

- Shopwell—Simplifies nutrition labels and helps you discover new foods that fit your lifestyle by providing personalized nutrition scores on scanned items based on dietary goals, health concerns, allergies, and dislikes.

- MyPlate—Track food/water intake and consumption habits and includes a tool for creating custom meal plans as well as a STRONGER fitness program that offers 30-minute workouts.

The Sitting Disease

Have you ever heard the expression "sitting is the new smoking"? Leading a sedentary lifestyle with little to no physical activity and/or primarily participating in activities where you sit or lie down (i.e., reading or watching TV) has become so common, particularly as we age, that it's been dubbed "The Sitting Disease."

Being sedentary can put you at higher risk for conditions such as high blood pressure, stroke, cardiovascular disease, some cancers, Type 2 diabetes, and even cognitive decline. What's more, bone loss may occur at a faster rate, you're more at risk for falls, and may have more trouble performing daily activities due to loss of muscle tissue. As if that isn't enough, you're also more at risk for depression.

So, get moving! Start with small steps and micro habits. Each month or two, add something new or increase your reps or distance. This is not a sprint, nor are you training for the Olympics. Slow and steady wins the race to mobility and extended health.

CHAPTER RESOURCES

- Visit www.payingforlongtermcare.com/meals for a list of meal planning and meal delivery services in your area
- Download a printable calendar for tracking daily exercise and nutrition at www.payingforlongtermcare.com/health

CHAPTER 17

Planning for Your Future

At this point it should be clear that long-term care issues are a major and inevitable part of life for all of us. Millions of seniors and their families are currently struggling to acquire much-needed long-term care—millions of others will soon face the same reality.

This chapter discusses some of the ways that you can be proactive in safeguarding your own quality of life and minimizing financial risks for yourself and your family as you age. The reality is that long-term care will eventually affect all of our lives, regardless of whether we're prepared.

The time to plan for your own long-term care is now. Having the following strategies in place can help you prepare for your own needs as you age.

Buying a Long-Term Care Insurance Policy

Long-term care insurance may be difficult to navigate without expert assistance, but it's also one of the most effective ways to help protect your wealth when you or a loved one needs long-term care. On that note, the need for long-term care often arises when you least expect it. Purchasing your policy early (and making sure that you understand its terms) can provide invaluable funding—and peace of mind—when an unexpected health crisis occurs.

By covering many of the expenses that federal programs and other funding options generally will not, long-term care insurance can provide far more care options and preserve your standard of living.

According to AARP, the ideal age to start shopping for a policy (assuming that you're still healthy and eligible for coverage) is between 60 and 65. Why? Because you're not too young or too old: a still-affordable monthly premium coupled with a total premium savings can help make your policy purchase as cost-effective as possible.

It's in your best interest to talk with a trusted financial adviser before purchasing a long-term care policy to make sure you understand its terms—and that its terms are uniquely customized for you.

Opening a Health Savings Account

You can start saving money today by investing in your own healthcare with a health savings account, and by harnessing the power of compounding interest on this account for your future nest egg.

An HSA helps people with high-deductible healthcare plans cover out-of-pocket medical expenses, and it's one of the most powerful parts of a well-designed healthcare strategy. HSA contributions are deductible from your gross pay, which gives you a powerful tax deduction that could potentially even place you into a lower tax bracket. Your HSA account only grows and expands for your future healthcare needs: the funds in your account grow tax-free and this isn't a "use it or lose it" plan. These funds can also be used tax-free on qualified medical expenses. After you turn 59 ½, there's an option to withdraw the funds for non-healthcare expenses and then pay federal income taxes on it.

Setting up your HSA is easy (See Chapter Resources in Chapter 10: Health Savings Accounts). It may be a good idea to speak with a licensed broker who can review some options for you. In the end, doing some research may help you gain more money in interest, spend less in fees, and give you more control over your account. As a reminder, your health insurance must be an HSA approved plan.

Strategizing a Financial Plan

Planning financially for your needs as you age should be given just as much priority as planning for college, getting married, buying a home, or any other major life event. Without a plan to pay for your long-term care needs, a single major health issue could quickly deplete the savings you—or your children—have spent a lifetime building.

Pre-Planning Strategies

Insurance and annuity products play a critical role in planning for long-term care expenses. If you are in your 60s and planning for way down the road or in your 80s and planning for five years down the road, there are options that can transfer some of the risk of your long-term care needs to an insurance company, providing peace of mind.

Here are a few ideas:

Life insurance products, which were built to pay long-term care expenses more than paying a large death benefit. While there are numerous variations of these products, the most common example is the client makes a one-time payment to the insurance company, let's say $100,000. The product will guarantee that if you never need it for long-term care purposes, your heirs will get back at least $100,000; but if you need long-term care such as assisted living, home care, etc., that product will pay out anywhere from $100,000 to hundreds of thousands depending on the product, age, time you've held the product, features you choose, etc. These products are excellent for anyone who can afford to set aside a lump sum of money for their care needs and is in good health.

Annuities with long-term care provisions. Many annuity companies are now building into their products provisions to help pay for long-term care expenses. These features may be as simple as waiving any early withdrawal fees to doubling your income stream. Here is an example of how that might look:

John is 70 and healthy. He deposits $100,000 into an annuity with a lifetime income rider. His intention is to leave the account untouched until he needs some care. At age 85 he requires care, so he turns on the income stream. The company doubles his projected income, so he receives $46,000 per year for 2.5 years and then the company continues to pay out $23,000 per year as long as he lives. This could result in a significant return on investment with no stock market risk. These products can be a huge benefit to anyone with longevity in their family. Best of all, if he doesn't need care, his heirs will receive the entire value of the account when he passes.

There are numerous other options or variations on the ideas suggested above. The most important thing is to seek advice of someone who specializes in financial planning for long-term care. Ask your planner the following questions:

- How many have you helped qualify for Medicaid?
- How many people have you helped apply for the VA Aid and Attendance benefit?
- How many times in the past month have you talked to an assisted living community or home care agency for a client?

You will know right away if you have the right person. Even if you are planning for the future, if your planner isn't thinking about

Medicaid, Aid, and Attendance benefits and long-term care options when setting up your finances, it is time to move on to someone who does.

Maintaining a Healthy Lifestyle

Staying healthy allows you to continue enjoying an active and fulfilled life longer, and it doesn't need to be complicated.

Healthy aging simply requires focusing on habits such as proper nutrition, regular exercise, sufficient sleep, and hydration. People tend to enjoy investing in the latest fads, trends, and diets to lose weight without realizing that changing their lifestyle makes all the difference.

- *Proper Nutrition*: People tend to enjoy investing in the latest fads, trends and diets to lose weight without realizing that changing their lifestyle makes all the difference. Cook more meals at home. As we age, we tend to eat far more pre-prepared meals in restaurants, where we're often overserved with foods saturated in excess sodium and sugar.
- *Exercise*: This could be as simple as walking several days a week. It's also important to remember the importance of flexibility and stretching. Check out YouTube videos or apps for free classes and guides.
- *Staying Hydrated*: You may have heard your mother tell you that you need to drink eight glasses of water a day. As it turns out, she was right. There are many free apps that can help remind you to drink enough water throughout your day. Keep in mind that studies show a direct correlation between drinking sufficient amounts of water and weight loss.
- *Getting Enough Sleep*: A healthy diet and regular exercise will help to fuel better sleep in general. Everyone has their needed

number of hours each night. Regardless of your personal number, keep your sleep schedule consistent and try to go to bed within the same 30-minute timeframe each night.

All of these things combined can lead to more mobility and healthier aging as you get older.

CHAPTER RESOURCES

- Find experts in the long-term care insurance industry at www.payingforlongtermcare.com/care

CHAPTER 18

Lessons Learned

One of life's toughest transitions is becoming a parent to a loved one. This role reversal is always emotional, especially when it happens unexpectedly. After all, you've likely spent a lifetime with them looking after you.

My personal experience with Tom's in-home health care and long-term care taught me some hard lessons that I hope make your experience a little easier. And, if you take one thing from this book, it's the importance of planning ahead. When families are better informed and less anxious, they're able to make more effective life decisions alongside their loved ones. Use the guides in this book to lay a foundation and a plan that will ease your own journey. Planning for long-term care is not only one of the smartest decisions you can make, consider it a gift to your family.

I know that my children, Maddy and Charlie, will do whatever is necessary when I need long-term care someday. But I hate to think about putting them through what I experienced with Tom: the unknown, the guilt, the fear of making mistakes. It's simply not a responsibility that I want them to bear. Your family shouldn't have to guess your intentions if you're not able to tell them yourself, or scramble to find funding for your care last minute under duress.

We spend hours planning for vacations, dinner parties, and special events that we find important. The truth is that no one wants to think, plan, or talk about the aging of themselves or a loved one. I challenge you to make a commitment to your family and to yourself and have these conversations *now*. Use the resources in this book to stimulate meaningful discussions that move everyone involved toward a far less stressful transition to care in the future.

Like so many others, I learned the following takeaways the hard way:

- The importance of having conversations as a family before crisis mode hits
- That you can save time and heartache by connecting with experienced senior professionals who know what you're going through and know how to help
- That it's normal to feel overwhelmed
- That there are many options to pay for care
- The importance of identifying family assets early and sharing this information with other family members
- That knowing how to search for senior care can make all the difference
- That it's important for the whole family to be on the same page and how to do it
- That you should always include your aging loved one in the planning process

Share this book with your loved ones: with over 10,000 people turning 65 every day, the reality is that most of us will be faced with issues involving in-home health or long-term care in our lifetime.

I wish you the very best in your journey and I would love to hear how this book has helped you or your family. Please reach out to me anytime.

Ben Rao

www.linkedin.com/in/benrao
www.payingforlongtermcare.com
www.facebook.com/payingforlongtermcare

I encourage you to leave an honest review on Amazon, as this helps other readers find the best resources for their family's needs.

ADDITIONAL RESOURCES

Elder Law Attorneys

    To find an elder law attorney in your area, visit www.payingforlongtermcare.com/ela

Overview of Senior Living Options

    For a list of senior care professionals in your area, visit www.payingforlongtermcare.com/pro

Staying at Home vs. Moving into a Senior Community

    Download a printable checklist to complete a senior safety home walk-through at www.payingforlongtermcare.com/safety

    Calculate the costs of staying at home vs. transitioning to a care community at www.payingforlongtermcare.com/calc

    Access expanded resources for recognizing warning signs in your aging loved one at www.payforlongtermcare.com/signs

    Find in-home care services in your area at www.payingforlongtermcare.com/home

The Cost of Long-Term Care

    Find the 2020 average costs of long-term care in your state at www.payingforlongtermcare.com/costs

Understanding Medicare/Medicaid

Find a certified medicaid planner in your area at www.payingforlongtermcare.com/plan

Identifying Family Assets and Financial Resources

Download a helpful guide to calculate your family's assets at www.payingforlongtermcare.com/assets

Selling the Family Home

Download a checklist for getting your house ready to sell at www.payingforlongtermcare.com/guide

Find resources to help you sell your house at www.payingforlongtermcare.com/sell

Veterans Benefits

For more information about how to apply and/or to find an accredited representative, visit www.payingforlongtermcare.com/vet

Long-Term Care Insurance

Learn the most common mistakes made by families during the claims process at www.payingforlongtermcare.com/claim

Receive a free review of your long-term care insurance policy with expert feedback and advice at www.payingforlongtermcare.com/review

Financial Resources for People with Cancer

Download a three-minute questionnaire to learn whether you may qualify for compensation from cancer trust funds at www.payingforlongtermcare.com/fund

Reverse Mortgages

Find an FHA-approved HECM lender in your area at www.payingforlongtermcare.com/reverse-mortgages

Additional Resources

Health Savings Accounts

Download the questions you need to ask your health insurance company to understand if you qualify for an HSA and find HSA providers in your area at www.payingforlongtermcare/hsa

Funding Strategies to Pay for Immediate Needs

Find a bridge loan lender in your area at www.payingforlongtermcare.com/bridge

Learn the questions that you should ask your financial planner at www.payingforlongtermcare.com/planners

Researching Senior Living Options

Evaluate your loved one's care needs with a customized online assessment tool at www.payingforlongtermcare.com/assessment

Download a printable care community comparison sheet at www.payingforlongtermcare.com/comparison

How Technology Can Help with Companionship and Safety

Find innovative senior safety and companionship apps at www.payingforlongtermcare.com/connect

Healthy Aging Through Nutrition and Exercise for Seniors

Visit www.payingforlongtermcare.com/meals for a list of meal planning and delivery services in your area

Find a printable calendar for tracking daily exercise and nutrition at www.payingforlongtermcare.com/health

Planning For Your Future

Find experts in the long-term care insurance industry at www.payingforlongtermcare.com/care

About the Author

BEN RAO is an author, life-long entrepreneur, philanthropist and senior care advocate who lives in Lee's Summit, Missouri.

Ben was born and raised in Louisville, Kentucky by his stepfather Tom and his mother Peela, who devoted 40 years in not-for-profit senior services. Ben experienced first-hand the emotional and financial struggle that families face when he was unexpectedly confronted with the reality of transitioning Tom into senior care. He was challenged by the lack of direction and resources available for a process that nearly all of us will eventually need to go through. That experience inspired Ben to use his personal and professional experience in the long-term care industry to help families transition their loved ones into senior care.

Ben lives with his wife, Rhonda, and their two children, Maddy and Charlie, in a renovated historic building that was once the Lee's Summit Hospital and the Dayton Hotel in Downtown Lee's Summit. He developed Lee's Summit's first entrepreneurial incubator and office space in a formerly vacant post office. He works there alongside his trusty sidekick, Charlie dog, a border collie who has gone to the office with him every day for the last 10 years. For more information about Ben and this book, please visit www.payingforlongtermcare.com.

Made in United States
North Haven, CT
08 March 2024

49701344R00104